UNVEILING THE MYSTERIES

OF THE CELESTIAL

AND ENGAGING

THE BLUEPRINT OF GOD

UNVEILING THE MYSTERIES OF THE CELESTIAL

AND ENGAGING THE BLUEPRINT OF GOD

Corina Pataki

Copyright © 2020 Corina Pataki
All rights reserved.
ISBN-13: 9798589185669

FORWARD

Do you know the story of Elisha and his servant? The one in 2nd Kings, where the prophet Elisha is surrounded by an army, and his servant is terrified? You might recall the moment he goes to tell Elisha the news, and Elisha responds with, "Not to worry, there's more with us than there are with them." Then Elisha prays to the Lord for his servant's eyes to be opened, and then he can finally see what Elisha sees – that there are angels all around them, far outnumbering that of the enemy.

I think reading a book like this is a lot like sitting around Elisha when he prays for the servant's eyes to be opened. Elisha could see, but he wanted his servant to see too. Corina can see, and she wants you to see too.

This book, which is a collection of experiences, teachings, and practices that Corina has observed from a heavenly perspective are designed to do just that. It's all designed so that your eyes will be opened to fulfill your divine purpose, so that you can take part in a heavenly perspective, and so that you can embark on a journey into God that will never stop growing.

There's such a need for this these days (and I'm sure that was true in Elisha's day as well). At a time when it seems society around us is clamoring for us to look down, down, down into a lower realm of thinking, feeling, and believing, this book is begging you to look up, to allow your whole consciousness to take on new meaning. Couldn't we all use an unveiling of celestial mysteries right now? Couldn't we all take a look at our eternal blueprint hidden for us in Christ?

I certainly need it. And it's with no exaggeration at all that I can tell you of the moment that I first heard Corina teach on our divine blueprint. It was at a home gathering in central Florida, and my wife and I had stolen away for an impromptu date night (I know, driving to hear a speaker doesn't sound that romantic does it, but that should give you an indication of how much Melissa and I wanted to hear Corina's message). When Corina started teaching of the blueprint of our lives, my wife and I were both in awe of what God was revealing to us. Seeing our journey – and our future – through this cosmic lens was a watershed moment in our lives. You might say that God "opened our eyes" like He did Elisha's servant.

Now, you get to read through this treasure trove of revelation and find out for yourself how your eyes can be opened. You get to determine (and this really is up to you) how much you will let God redefine your purpose and your relationship with Him. When you read Corina's words you're going to see again and again as I did, that she is determined to get you to step into that high calling that Christ has given you. I hope you dive in without hesitation, because you are needed for such a time as this.

Christopher Paul Carter
Discover the Heavens

12/17/2020

UNVEILING THE MYSTERIES OF THE CELESTIAL AND ENGAGING THE BLUEPRINT OF GOD

INTRODUCTION

The Lord is wanting to take us through a process of maturity, so that we can be present back to Him as mature sons that are THEN ready to be anointed as kings, out of our mature sonship position. Then, we can be appointed as priests, under the Order of Melchizedek in order to take dominion over the earth, to cleanse the heavens and establish His kingdom government in all of creation! Before this can happen, first and foremost, it starts with us really getting to know, understand, and see who we really are and all that He has given us access to have, walk into, and release out. With that knowledge in hand, it is crucial for us to deal with our junk by applying the full benefits that He gave to us as He continues to unveil these mysteries for such a time as this to whoever desires to engage them and walk out the process on a daily basis.

With this being said, I believe that there are a few very powerful tools and foundational revelations that YHVH has released that should be a MUST for us to take in, understand, and apply if not on a daily basis, AS OFTEN AS POSSIBLE! The Word says that His people perish due to a lack of knowledge. Well, the knowledge and understanding of the mysteries that have been hidden for generations and ages, from man, and angels have been unlocked! It is our individual choice if we will go seek it out, or stay in our comfort place, satisfied with what we have.

If you are one that is not satisfied with where you are, with what you are walking out and displaying, with where your family is ... if you are one that hungers for "the more", keep reading!

Now, let's go back to those foundational revelations that I believe is a must for all that want to go deeper. First, I believe that we MUST learn and understand about Trading Floors. The demonic ones first...what they are, how they affect us, how one gets on them, how to get off of them, and how to stay off of them. Then we must learn about the Heavenly Trading Floors, what they are and how we can begin to trade on those trading floors and the outcome that takes place as a result, not only in us as individuals, but, to our entire DNA/bloodline!

Another EXTREMELY powerful and much needed foundational revelation, tool and principal that He has revealed is the mystery of communion. WOW, WOW...what a powerful and HUGELY needed revelation this is! This has the power to literally transform our mutated, twisted, carnal, mortal, mixed, DNA into the DNA of YHVH...the same DNA that Jesus carries!

Communion is not supposed to be just something we do, maybe once a month to remember His sacrifice...though remembering is part of it. Communion is so much more than that! It is us applying the FINISHED work of the cross...did you see the word, "FINISHED"? Finished means done, completed, ended, already done. NOT "it will be done at some point in the future, when I die and go in my home... by and by." Another part to this mystery of communion is the understanding of us not stopping at the cross but realizing that the cross is a GATEWAY into the next that Jesus gave us access to, because of His sacrifice on the cross! Resurrection Life and Resurrection Power NOW in this world, not when we die! Death should NOT EVEN HAVE A STING! Listen, we are supposed to be incorruptible, immortal spirit beings, walking with EVERLASTING LIFE, NOW!!! That is what Jesus gave us THROUGH the cross. That is the trade that He did on our behalf, that gives us the ability to take our mutated and corrupted DNA, the DNA of our entire bloodline and trade it for His finished work, for the record of His DNA, that is found in His blood! No matter how corrupt your DNA is, don't lose heart! There is a plan that has been hidden before the ages, but NOW, God is revealing it to the spiritually mature ones who are ripe and ready IN their understanding!

Let's continue. After you begin to understand Trading Floors and you begin to be DILIGENT by CHOOSING to start getting off of the demonic Trading Floors, don't stop there! After getting the understanding of having access to step into the celestial and engage the blueprint of God, the original one that He has prepared for you, don't stop there! After getting the knowledge of Communion, engaging in that, and also CHOOSING to be DILIGENT, engaging in all these foundational revelations as often as possible, THEN, YOU WILL BEGIN TO CHANGE, from the inside out! Now, the Father is ready to release to you, in you and through you the MORE that He has, again, not only for you, but for your entire bloodline...including your children and all future generations!

You see, with the Lord, there are layers of revelation...steppingstones, if you will. One foundational revelation will become your steppingstone or ceiling that will take you to the next level, if you choose to step on it. It is line upon line and precept upon precept. The Lord spoke to me about these foundations that I must teach on, for whosoever chooses to engage with them. I was told to write books on these foundational "musts" so that all who read it can begin to step UP into what He has for them. We must go from glory to glory. One level of revelation to the other. However, we have to have foundations so that we can stand on them, before we step to the next level of foundation! We must learn the material and apply its teaching in a tangible way at each level we find ourselves.

With this in mind, The Lord, with the strong encouragement from Wendy, my bff, I started, and I am in the process of writing the 1st series of these books called Becoming the Shining ones, Sons of light...Foundational Revelation for your Transformation. There will be three books in this first series. These books will reveal and teach the reader these three very crucial foundational revelations that must become principals in our lives, if we want to see transformation and transfiguration. The first book in this series is already available...Unveiling the Trading Floors and Stepping into the Order of Melchizedek. This book is the 2nd book in this series and there will be the third book called, Unveiling the Mysteries of Communion.

Why was the Lord so specific with me on the order of these books? You see, you cannot walk out your original blueprint as long as you are on demonic trading floors and trading with these principalities! You FIRST MUST start taking away the legal rights of these demonic principalities by understanding Trading and applying the knowledge, council and revelation of this huge principal. If you do not have, first, the understanding of Trading Floors, the enemy has full access to come and steal your God given inheritance, because of the trades made on their demonic floors. Therefore, all that you are supposed to walk in, the inheritance that God put in your original blueprint, will be stolen and lost, legally! God will not allow that! It's like you as a parent not yet giving your little child something that you know he or she is not mature enough to receive, and to carry, because you know that it may be lost or stolen. Same with The Lord.

The second reason that you will not be able to walk out your original blueprint is because God is a God of rules, principles, and order. Listen, the Kingdom of God will NOT come upon ANYTHING THAT DOES NOT LOOK LIKE IT! Therefore, we must become a shadow of the reflection of Him and His kingdom. So, when He looks for a shadow of Himself, He will see it IN YOU, and He can then begin to release through you, all that He has for you! At that point, He knows that the enemy has no legal right to it since you are now a reflection of Adonai, and there is no longer anything in you that is of the enemy! I will explain this deeper in the chapters to follow.

Jesus prayed that the Kingdom of Heaven would come and be reflected on earth, as it is in Heaven. How is that going to happen? Through you and me! God wants, as I said above, for His Kingdom to come upon and in us, and be reflected through us, everywhere we go! However, again, the Kingdom of Heaven will not come upon anything that does not look like it! Let me say it again, We MUST create a shadow of HIM...so that He can see it, and release EVERYTHING that He is, and everything that He has for us, including our original blueprint, in our DNA, our bloodline, our family, our city, or state, our nation, earth, and in all of creation! I will break this down a bit later.

Now, after you have the foundational principle and understanding of the Trading Floors and you are diligent in dealing with that, it is CRUCIAL that you have the foundational understanding of what communion really is and start to engage with that! As you combine communion, the new understanding of what it really is, and what it really does to you and for you, as you are getting off the demonic trading floors AND going into your Father's Kingdom to see and get your original blueprint, you are on your way to freedom! Wow, wow, WOW!

Now, for those of you that never hear me speak, or have never read any of my books, please know that I repeat myself a lot! My purpose for teaching, speaking, writing books is not to show you how much I know. My biggest desire is that whoever hears or reads these teachings, GETS IT, applies it and becomes changed! I will repeat a point as much as The Lord tells me to repeat it, until all the ones that hear me, or read these books, get it. So, I more than likely may say the same thing again, maybe in a different way, as He leads me because my desire is that all who read these books will get an understanding, applying it by faith, and seeing a tangible transformation!

I am also HUGE on honor and I always want to make sure to give honor where honor is due. I would like to honor the incredible forerunner of this magnificent "new move" … "the more" of YHVH. He has chosen to pay the price for not only walking out these new paths, trailblazing with Adonai, but he has chosen to teach, traveling around the world, to whosoever was hungry for "the more" that YHVH has. THANK YOU, Ian Clayton, for all the sacrifices you made to be a true trailblazer, a general, and a father to challenge the sons to come up and step into the reality of ALL that He has for us, as sons. Steve and I honor and love both you and Kay!

I also want to honor Wendy Cooper Porcelli for being my sister (blue blood sister - wink wink), my best friend, my confidant, the superb help from Yeshua, the incredible machine of Kingdom Reflections and every branch of it, for dreaming with me and believing in me and all that God has in His heart for Kingdom Reflections to do, as well as us! Thank you for encouraging me to write these books and for taking on the "battle" to get them ready and put them out there. I love you!

THE VIOLENT TAKE IT BY FORCE

Let's begin! Let me mention one thing from the beginning that is very important for us to understand. Everything you read in this book, or in the Trading Floors book ... everything you are learning to do, engage in, and apply ... does not mean that you do it once or twice or maybe three times and you stop! Hear me, please... doing these things a few times does not mean that you walk in the fullness of the victory. Listen, let's look at the Trading Floors. Those Trading Floors have been traded on for thousands and thousands, and tens of thousands of years! You will not have the full victory over them the first time, or the second time...you must do it until you see complete victory, no matter how long it takes! How much freedom you get is contingent on how serious you are, and how bad you want that complete freedom! How deep do you want to clean your bloodline?

Ladies, maybe some of you will understand this analogy. Maybe some of you guys will also understand it. How deep you want to clean your house? I mean, seriously, if you just want to clean superficially kind of like wipe the dust around the stuff you have on the furniture, you can do that! Or, if you just want to vacuum and dust and maybe clean the kitchen counter and that's it. That is your choice and that is fine! Or maybe you want to do all of that AND get down on and scrub the floors. You can apply that as a spiritual aspect, in all that you are reading and learning. According to your determination and tenacity [for the total freedom of your bloodline] will determine your victory. Why? Because, if you are determined to go deeper and deeper, and find every nook and cranny where the enemy has been hiding, stealing, creating violence in every form ... if you want to know how, why, and what he has been trading on in your bloodline ... if you are tenacious to find all legal rights, as the Father wants to show you, to annihilate them by and through the blood of YESHUA, to take it by force, let me tell you then, VICTORY IS YOURS!

The Word says that the Kingdom of God suffers violence, BUT the violent take it by force! Where is the Kingdom of God supposed to be? In you! The Kingdom of the Earth is all that you see here on the earth, but the Kingdom of God is supposed to be inside your spirit man and the Kingdom of Heaven is at hand ... it is the abode of YHVH. It is at hand. In the Hebrew mindset, it is as close to you as the air that you breathe! So, when we read that the Kingdom of God suffers violence, what does that mean? Since the Kingdom of God is in you. What this is saying is that there has been violence that has come against YOU and your bloodline...through legal rights, thievery, trading, binding documents, agreements, whatever they may be. However, The Lord is trying to tell you that, though you and your bloodline have suffered violence, you must take it by force! Notice, it is not a suggestion but a declaration. The choice is ours. So, what does it mean to take it by force? It means that we must realize who we are and what we have inside of us. Next, we must engage with that and let the Spirit of Might, the Spirit of the Fear of The Lord, and the Vengeance of The Lord operate THROUGH you, as the cry of the Lion of Judah is released out of you...that warrior that is inside of you and then, TAKE IT ALL BY FORCE! IT IS YOURS!!!

However deep you want to *go;* He will take you. However much you want Him to show you, that's how much He will show you! How much freedom do you want? The trading that you put in, is the value of multiplication and freedom that you get out. Listen, the reality is that you could easily spend one year on one trading floor because, again, these trading floors have been traded on for tens of thousands of years. HOWEVER, "Today starts my first day of freedom for my entire bloodline and even if I receive one percent of the victory today and, tomorrow, another one percent, I AM WALKING in more victory and freedom today than I did yesterday!" The point is that you are walking your freedom out, you are receiving more of your blueprint today than you had yesterday!

I would like you to remember this very important point that I will continue to make in this book, that I stress in my teachings ... DO NOT STOP ... DO NOT PARK AT ANY ONE PLACE, REVELATION, ENCOUNTER, VICTORY, GLORY REALM BUT, RATHER, KEEP GOING!! We are supposed to go from glory to glory! YHVH never stops...He is always on the move! We are only supposed to stop long enough to learn, engage, apply and then go on to the next move, the next step of glory, teaching, revelation, mystery, victory that He has for us! How bad do you want to see, engage and operate out of your original blueprint?

Whatever you have authority over, you are responsible for. So, then, because you were given the authority to go on the demonic trading floors, and to start getting off of them, you are now responsible to keep going back, checking the ground that you took. You are responsible to continue to walk out the victory and the freedom that you are receiving, for you and your entire bloodline. I know sometimes we go to meetings and we have an encounter and then, we think that, because we did that one encounter, we now walk in the total victory. We go about our daily lives, forgetting our responsibility because we are not yet mature (since maturity is a process), and we fall back into complacency. Then, we are shocked and wonder why we see so little victory, if anything. This is because, though we have the authority, we were not responsible to look after what was entrusted to us ... the victory and the ground won. Let me give you an example. A good, mature, wise, and responsible king, once he conquers a land, will know that he is now responsible for it. He is responsible to keep going back to check the land. He is responsible to feed the people, to make sure that the land produces what it needs to produce, and to make sure that the enemy, who was defeated, does not return again, bringing a bigger army, stealing back the land.

We must come up IN our maturity level. This means we must do more than just the few things that we have been doing or doing what we are led to do in a meeting and stopping there. We must come out of the mentality of doing something once or twice, or a few times, and, after, thinking, "Oh it's done, Jesus, thank you. Now everything will completely change, and I have nothing more to do. I'm done." Listen, can God do it just like that all at once? Of course, He can! However, He is after raising mature sons who know who they are, know how to stand, know how to fight, know how to be fearless, know how to be bold, and know how to be persistent. He is not wanting to raise spoiled brats who get everything they want handed to them. Do you get what

I am saying? I am saying this with LOTS of love and hugs and much honey smeared on these words.

The activation we will do at the end of this book, as well as the activation we did at the end of the Trading Floors book, is to, first of all, show you how to do it. It is also to show you that you can do it; and to activate your spiritual sight and encourage you to keep going deeper and higher! Remember, don't just do it once or twice. Do it as often as possible! How bad you want it is determined by the effort you put in it, and the time you spend engaging. Hopefully, as you do the activation many times, you will see the wonders of what He has given you access to step into. As you do that, THAT will create a hunger and a determination in you to build a stronger relationship with Jesus, with The Father, The Holy Spirit and all the beings He has surrounding you that are part of your blueprint!

INVITATION FOR THE CHOSEN

The very first time I heard anyone mention blueprints was Ian Clayton. I was absolutely blown away by this revelation which The Lord was revealing through Ian. As I heard it, I grabbed it like a bull by the horns, and I went before The Father as I always do (when I want to see, understand, and walk into the next level of what He has in any given revelation).

I am going to pause here to say this ... You see, the reason The Lord gives a revelation through a person is not for us to stop at that revelation, look in awe and wonder at that revelation, build a theology on that revelation, or create idols of the people who the revelation was released through. The Lord releases those revelations through forerunners such as Ian, and others, so that we can now realize that we can also engage that revelation and go deeper and higher in it ... to go beyond! Let me give you an example. You see, The Lord used Ian at different times to show me a door, if you will, through the revelations that The Father gave him; the revelations that he was willing to release. I then CHOSE to go THROUGH that door of revelation that God used Ian to open, going into the MORE that Adonai has for ME, my children, and my entire bloodline. Why? Because of my desire for MORE OF HIM ... my desire to go past the limitations of the boundaries that religious spirits and doctrines taught to me since I was small. Not only that, but now every "door" of revelation He has me open, as a trailblazer and a forerunner in the arena He has entrusted me, is now an invitation for YOU! It now becomes an invitation for whosoever CHOOSES to enter in themselves ... For whosoever will allow the Father to take them deeper and higher so that, in turn, they can become that door for others! Remember we are gates and portals! What are you choosing to release out of your gate/portal? IF we all did that, we, as His sons, would grow in our maturity process, going from glory to glory, and we would truly become unstoppable! Why? Because whatever you are in the presence of, whatever you look to, whatever you focus on, multiplies in and for you. Also, whatever you focus on, whatever you are in the presence of, you become like, and that is what will be reflected in and through you, in every situation, in every arena you are in.

So, in this book, I will try to unpack these amazing and powerful revelations that I firmly believe, if applied as often as He leads you, will change the trajectory not only of your life but of your bloodline and seedline. How? These amazing revelations will teach you how to live out of your ORIGINAL blueprint, therefore, enabling you to walk out your ORIGINAL destiny scroll, bringing that trajectory change to your entire generational line!

In this book, we will look at what a blueprint is, what a destiny scroll is, what the difference between the two is, and we will learn to question if are we really living our original blueprint and walking out our original destiny scroll? What does that mean? What is the voice of the celestial? We will look at Abraham and his birth, his early years and what he has to do with this amazing revelation and ohhh...so many more mysteries that He is revealing in this book!

For the ones that have never heard me before, or who have never read my books before, I always start out with these very amazingly powerful truths that most of us in the western world have not heard of. For those of you who have heard me before or who have read my books, you will hear this again, which is good because it reinforces these truths in your brain.

Now, let me say this, Jesus spoke Aramaic. All His disciples were Hebrew, speaking Aramaic...correct? None of them were Greek, though some of them could speak it. So, watch this amazing fact; The Rabbis say that God is so amazing that He chose to reveal Himself in the language of men. Now, what they say is that one word of God, just one word, is like a diamond that has 70 different facets! According to how the Spirit of Revelation hits one of those facets, out of the 70 facets found in one word, is what God is trying to tell you and me through that one word!

Now, going deeper, one scripture has four different understandings, with four different applications. Each understanding has 70 different facets. So here we are thinking we went to seminary for two, four, or ten years and, because we know that this is what the

Greek says, because that is what we learned and what we have been taught, this is the totality of what God is speaking to us. If anybody else tries to come along with anything else, they're considered heretics! Please hear me, seminary is GREAT, but it is only to give us a foundation of understanding from a soulish perspective. Why are you stopping there? It is head knowledge...why are you stopping there? On that foundation, God wants to build and expand His revelatory knowledge that He releases to our spirit man, so that we can grow in experiential knowledge of who He is and who we REALLY are. It is NOT supposed to be an end-all, but a beginning, a jumping off platform!

Listen, God is on the move. It's all about revelations, not about tradition! Tradition makes you look in the past at what God DID back then. Tradition is what you have learned from your pastor, from your grandma, your parents, or Sister Sue! It always makes you look in the rearview mirror. Unfortunately, tradition has NO USE for a deeper, personal relationship with Jesus. Why? Because, number one, it only relies on the teachings of the past, the teachings of the forefathers, what everyone has taught us, what we heard, "what my pastor told me". They become historical facts that we limit ourselves to and build a traditional Christianity upon. Is that really all that Jesus came to give to us? You see, all of these traditions that we hold on to excuses and eliminates the need to "search God for MYSELF", to see and hear what He has for us to see, to tap into, to do, to understand, and to engage. We walk around saying, "I am just going to rely on the traditions I have been taught because I am not willing to leave my comfort zone and spend the time to seek Him for myself." Again, traditions also ALWAYS make you look behind, in the past, in the rearview mirror where you can miss what God has in front of you, in this time, and for this season. Traditions are a demonic tool that keep people who choose to stay there, BOUND to the past. Therefore, then, they bound to generational curses, trading that was done on demonic trading floors, and all the limitations of their past generations, creating a chaotic and limited reality that they are continuously walking in, generation after generation!

Revelation, on the other hand, makes you look forward and pushes you to SEEK Him out for what He has next for you! God is always on the move, wanting us to follow Him. Remember, we are supposed to go from glory to glory to glory, from one step of maturity, one level of transformation into the next, until we are transformed into that new CREATION that we are supposed to be NOW, not when we die! We are supposed to walk a reality that has NO limitations, living outside of time and space and all laws which have bound us to human limitations. For I can do ALL things through Christ Jesus for, now, ALL things ARE POSSIBLE! This means, keep moving until our perfection is complete and THEN, KEEP MOVING INTO THE NEXT! We are not supposed to stop and build memorials around the past moves of God, being stuck there, trying to copy the "formulas" of what they did so that we can achieve what they achieved. We must not stop at wanting JUST to bring the past experiences into our present, but we must desire to build on their ceiling, to build on where they left off. To go higher than they have gone, reaching forward, towards the high call of God, that He has for us to step into! That means, we must learn to live OUT OF the age to come, which means NOT living from our past, but from our future! Paul reached forward, through his present, into the future, as he grabbed a hold of the high call that God had for him. We must do the same.

Now, to move on. The word of God is living, and it is breathing. You guys, the Bible says that His word is alive, breathing, pulsating. It is not just black or red words on white paper. These words are ALIVE! Therefore, however deep you want to go IN His word, His WORD will begin to unfold itself and invite you to step IN, see beyond what you have seen before, and go beyond where you have gone before!

You see, God is a multidimensional God, and His word is a multidimensional word. Again, depending on how deep you want to go in it, the Word will unfold and take you IN its multidimensional levels of the revelation, of what God is wanting to unveil to you, in any scripture or story that you are reading. If you want to stay at one level, that is ok! But, if you want to go deeper, GET READY!

You see, the Bible is not just a book of amazing stories and historical events. The Bible is an INVITATION for whosoever [will] to go beyond the places, beyond space and time, and encounter what is read! You guys, I want to drive this into your spirit, the word of God IS ALIVE!!!!!!!!!! The Hebrew letters are all living individual beings ready to take you into the mysteries that they hold of our Father, but it is up to you and to me how bad we want it!

Let me also say that these revelations unveiled in this book have nothing to do with salvation! If you received the Lord Jesus Christ into your life and your heart, you are saved and born again. If and when you die, you will go to Heaven and not to hell. However, these revelations that I am bringing forth in this book are for the ones that desire the MORE. These are for the ones that KNOW that there is so much more that Jesus talked about which we are supposed to do and become while on the earth. This book is for the ones who want to discover these mysteries and revelations … who want to tap into them and to start manifesting the fullness of what the Bible says we are supposed to manifest.

You see, the cross is the very beginning! You cannot walk into anything that I will talk about in this book if you have not gone, first, at the cross. HOWEVER, we MUST NOT stop at the cross, but we must go THROUGH THE CROSS into all the benefits which Jesus gave to us, which is for NOW, not when we die!!! Remember what Proverbs 25:2 in TPT (Passion Translation) says, "God conceals the REVELATION of His word in the hiding place of His glory. But the honor of kings [maturity of the kings] is revealed by how they THOROUGHLY search out the DEEPER meaning of ALL the God says." In a different translation, it states that it is the Glory of God to HIDE a MYSTERY and it is for the MATURITY OF THE KINGS TO SEARCH THEM OUT!

So, let's break this scripture down a bit, because we have heard it quoted so much and, yet, what does it really mean? YHVH hides the mysteries of His word (which, again, are NOT black or red words on white paper ... they are LIVING BEINGS), and the revelation that is found in those mysteries, IN those Words. The access to those mysteries, the access into the place of "hiding/hidden" is IN the place of His glory. That is not for everyone. It's for the sons. Is it for the immature lazy ones? No. It is for the ones who have CHOSEN to go THROUGH the process of maturity that are then ready to be presented to the Father as matured sons and, out of that position, to be anointed as kings. So, they have become kings out of their sonship position.

Now, honor and maturity go hand in hand. You cannot have one without the other because you obviously cannot be honored as a king that is FIRST a mature son, without that maturity. A son can ONLY be honored to step into the position of a king, through maturity. A king's honor can ONLY be seen by God and others through the maturity of UNDERSTANDING his/her role as a king. One of those very important roles IS ... THOROUGHLY searching out the deeper meaning or mysteries of ALL God has hidden, that is beyond the veil, that is in the dark cloud of His glory, which is ONLY found IN AND THROUGH His heart ... In other words, RELATIONSHIP, RELATIONSHIP, RELATIONSHIP!

Remember, Jesus Himself said that ALL the things that He did, we must do. Let's just remember a few of those things. He walked on water, walked through walls, walked through people, created matter out of nothing, raised the dead, healed the sick ... These are just a few things that the Bible tells us about. However, remember that He said that all the things He did are NOT written down because, if they would have been written down, there would not be ... NOT BE ENOUGH LIBRARIES IN THE WORLD to contain ALL the things He did. Now, let us just revisit this statement about all that He did, again, just to make sure that we are understanding what Jesus is really telling us here. So, again, He said that we HAVE to do ALL the things that He did, not only the ones we have read about in the Bible, but, rather, ALL the things that He did that are not written down ... AND, yet

GREATER things! Now, have you ever seen the Library of Congress, or the biggest Library in Chicago, or the one in the Vatican? They are HUGE! However, Jesus says that in ALL the world, there would not be enough LIBRARIES TO CONTAIN ALL THAT HE DID and, again, we are NOT ONLY TO DO ALL THAT ... BUT THE M O R E! Are you kidding me??!?? Look how low we have been operating! Why? Because of the lies and control of the demonic, religious system working hand in hand with antichrist spirits that have programmed us, programmed our belief systems, IN FEAR, MANIPULATION, AND CONTROL. As we engaged in those lies, we made agreements and covenants through choices we made which created a chaotic, mutated reality that IS NOT mirroring God's ORIGINAL blueprint and the FULL VICTORY Jesus gave us at the cross and THROUGH the cross! That programing, and fear-based control, has also lulled us in a spiritual amnesia that has put our consciousness in a place of complacency and comfort ... laziness, lacking the desire to wake up, to mature, to sacrifice our comforts, creating a lack for a true, deep desire to build a deeper relationship with the Godhead, our God family...on our own, with NO MIDDLEMAN NEED!

Okay, let's look at this scripture with which I always love to start these teachings. 1 Corinthians Chapter 2:6, AMP "Yet when we are among the fully grown, spiritually mature Christians, who are RIPE IN their understanding, we do impart a higher wisdom, the knowledge of the divine plan previously hidden, and it is not a wisdom of this age or this world."

Make sure you are connecting with this scripture because Paul is trying to tell us some deep stuff here: "Rather what we are setting forth is a wisdom of God once hidden from human understanding, human scrutiny and NOW revealed by God... that wisdom that was decreed before the ages."

What is this wisdom that he's talking about? What is the purpose of it? Look what it's saying. This wisdom that He is talking about, is a wisdom that is revealing to us, in THE DIVINE PLAN, decreed before the ages, and it was at one time hidden but now, it is revealed to the spiritually mature ones. Again, what is the purpose of this wisdom? It's for our glorification ... to lift us up [NOW] into THE GLORY OF HIS PRESENCE! It's not for when we die! Listen, He does not need you and me to understand these mysteries, and this excellent plan that has been previously hidden, after we die! When we go in heaven ... when we go past the veil, on the other side ... when we die (if you choose to believe that you will die), we don't have to battle anything! Therefore, after death, when we go to Heaven, there are no deep, mysterious plans He needs us to know about that will enable our transformation into all that He wants us to become; so that we can do all that He said we are to do! No! God needs His sons to wake up now and step into the fullness of everything that Jesus gave on the cross.

We must step into all that He made a way for us to step into, through the cross, to be lifted up into His presence NOW, so that we can be transformed and look like Him ... glorified, reflecting, and manifesting THAT on the earth and in all of creation!

Like I said earlier, whatever you look to, you become like. Whatever you are in the presence of, you take on its essence. So, when we are lifted up into His presence, we become like He is, "glorified"! He needs us to become that NOW, because ALL of creation is waiting with ANTICIPATION...we have a big job to do!

So, as we are LIFTED UP, we become glorified, because as we are lifted up in our position looking at Him and we start looking like Him. Not only that, but we are now also releasing THAT image and THAT power on the earth and in all of creation: As we do that, look what it says ... this scripture that we have all heard, and we have quoted without REALLY understanding the next dimension of it is. So, after you are lifted up and you start to look and act LIKE HIM...

V. 9 "For what eye has NOT seen, and ear has NOT heard, it has NEVER entered into the heart of men ALL that God has [PAST tense...already prepared] prepared for (1) those who love Him, (2) who hold Him in affection, (3) who obey Him and (4) RECOGNIZING the FULL benefits that He has bestowed upon us."

Okay, let's really grasp what this is saying. So, NO EYE HAS EVER, EVER seen (not even Enoch has seen these things)! Of ALL of the amazing things that Enoch did see, still, not even he has seen these things ... Even his eyes have NOT seen! Moses has not seen them. Elijah has not seen them. Isaiah has not seen them. David, Daniel, Adam ... none of these great men, these great generals, patriots have ever seen ... have EVER HEARD OR COMPREHENDED THESE THINGS THAT GOD HAS PREPARED! Do you understand? This is huge! Who has He prepared them for?

Let's look a bit deeper. It says, "... those things that God has prepared for ..." For whom? Here's the key. "... (1) for those that love Him, (2) who hold Him in affection, [relationship, relationship with Him] (3) obeying Him and (4) RECOGNIZING the FULL benefits that He has bestowed on us." Notice, this is NOT for everyone. This is for those who CHOOSE to do all these four things mentioned above in the scripture. God LOVES numbers! He speaks through numbers, so everywhere you see a number pattern in the scripture, PAY ATTENTION because He is trying to tell you something to unveil a mystery. Number one, we see it is to LOVE Him. The second key is "for the ones that hold Him in affection". The third one is "for the ones that choose to obey Him" and the fourth is for the ones who RECOGNIZE ALL (notice not part but ALL) the BENEFITS that He has bestowed on us! It is ALL about relationships! All these four qualifications are about relationships with Jesus, the Father, and the Holy Spirit.

Let's go even deeper with this one scripture. I am gonna break it down even more. As I said, God is huge with numbers. He speaks through numbers and He created numbers! Yes, the enemy uses numbers as well because he always steals what God created and he then perverts them and uses them for his benefit.

So, let me tell you a bit of how God speaks through numbers and I will just discuss numbers 2, 3, and 4. Now, in the Hebraic mindset and understanding, number 2 speaks of two points connecting, and forming an arc. It speaks of an agreement when two points connect, or two people connect as they form an arc over what they have agreed upon. So, when an arc is formed, the Father opens up a window in Heaven and pours down whatsoever the two have agreed upon!

Number 3 does not speak of a "three strand cord that cannot be easily broken" as we have been taught! The word "easily" is NOT in the original translation! How can the Father, the Son Yeshua, and Holy Spirit be broken IN ANY WAY; even if "not easily"? For just that word "broken" to be associated with the bond that YHVH, Yeshuah, and Rukha D'qudsha (Aramaic)/Ruach Ha Kodesh (Hebrew) have ... that it can possibly be broken ... is insane! Anyway, so the number 3 speaks of the three-strand cord that CAN NOT BE BROKEN, and it also speaks of the Bench of Three, The Father, Jesus, and Holy Spirit, standing together in the Courts of Heaven on your behalf!

Now, number 4 speaks not only of the four directions, or the four corners of the world, or of the four elements, BUT it also speaks of the name of GOD...YHVH ... Lion, Eagle, Ox, Man! The number 4 also speaks of a door or portal opening up in heaven giving entry to whosoever chooses to step in, through it!

So, watch this. When we love Him ... when we obey Him ... when we hold Him in affection and we recognize ALL the benefits that He gave to us, we have JUST STEPPED INTO THE NAME OF YHVH OUT OF OUR DESIRE TO BUILD RELATIONSHIP WITH HIM! Do you understand that when you do THESE THINGS, YOU, THEN, JUST RECEIVED ACCESS TO STEP INTO HIS NAME, WHICH IS A PORTAL; A DOOR FOR YOU TO STEP INTO THE FULLNESS THAT IS FOUND THROUGH HIS NAME!!!!! That means, ALL THE THINGS THAT ARE IN HIS NAME, ALL THE DIMENSIONS OF HEAVEN, ALL THE POWER OF THE LION, EAGLE, OX AND MAN... YOU NOW HAVE JUST STEPPED THROUGH IT ALL! You have JUST stepped into "NOW, I CAN DO ALL THINGS THROUGH CHRIST JESUS!" Oh, my goodness, I so feel His presence! Do you feel it as you are reading these TRUTHS and engaging with what Spirit of Truth is trying to show you? My...oh my! Woohoo!!

Let's go on to the next verse... "...yet to us, God unveiled and revealed them by and through the Holy Spirit." Watch this! "... for the Holy Spirit searches the sounding, (sound is frequency and vibration) of the profound and bottomless things of God where the DIVINE COUNCIL OF AND THINGS HIDDEN ARE that are far beyond human understanding."

Let me suggest to you that those bottomless things of God, where there is a frequency, a sound of these profound things and where there is a DIVINE COUNCIL OF things hidden, OR a Divine Council AND things hidden IS IN His HEART!

The Spirit of Truth is waiting to take us into the heart of YHVH where Mystery is ready to unveil those profound things that have been hidden, that are now waiting for someone who chooses relationship ... who chooses to not let anything stop them! These are the ones who CHOOSE to go in and have them unveiled and revealed to them, so that they can do things that NO ONE HAS EVER DONE, HAS EVER SEEN, HAS EVER HEARD, OR UNDERSTOOD.

I hope that you are noticing that we have stopped at so little! We have learned about The Cross and the importance of it and, let me make this clear, please, if I may... The Cross IS THE VERY BEGINNING! If you do not go TO THE CROSS, YOU CAN NOT GO THROUGH THE CROSS ... you can NOT have part in ANY of these things being discussed in this book. HOWEVER, we are NOT to stop at the cross! Many of us and many denominations have totally parked at The Cross, meaning, for them, The Cross IS IT, and, beyond that, it is all seen by them as "new age" or heresy. Oh, my goodness ... they are missing the FULL reason and ALL the benefits that He has given to us BECAUSE OF THE CROSS, and the ACCESS we have to GO THROUGH THE CROSS!

The Cross is the very beginning but now, we MUST realize that The Cross IS THE ENTRY POINT INTO THE FULL BENEFITS which can ONLY BE ACCESSED THROUGH THE CROSS! Do you understand?

Let me make this clear, again, this has NOTHING to do with salvation! IF you want to stop at salvation, at The Cross and you are satisfied with that, you are more than blessed to do so! THIS IS for the ones who KNOW that there is much more that Jesus gave us access to have THROUGH the Covenant of Adoption that He gave us THROUGH the Cross!

You see, at The Cross, as we get saved, the Spirit of Adoption comes in, by which we now have the ability to call Him "Abba Father". However, because, with The Lord, NOTHING STOPS, all is in a continual growth and expansion process, The Spirit of Adoption carries The Covenant of Adoption, which carries the totality of our inheritance! However, if we do NOT CHOOSE to go after what is in it, after the "more" that Jesus gave us access to STEP INTO, if we are just satisfied with our salvation and don't what the more (for whatever reason fear, comfort, lack of desire, satisfaction with our life), WE WILL NEVER STEP INTO THE THINGS THAT ARE IN THE COVENANT OF ADOPTION, BECAUSE WE STOPPED AT THE CROSS, AT SALVATION!

We can see, even in the Word, a clear picture of choices we have in order for us to step into the "more". Part of "the more" that we have access to is for us to be transformed into His image literally! Our choices make it possible for our mutated, corrupt DNA to be transformed and take on the image of His DNA, changing us on the inside, and transfiguring us on the outside, so that as He is for us to also become IN THIS WORLD, not when we die! It is not figurative, but literal!

Listen, I know that this is not for everyone! Why? Because there is a CHOICE attached to this! Yeshuah wants all these things to be for all, and He has made it available for all, but it requires a choice to be made. Just because you are saved, and chose to stop at the Cross, does not mean you will be transformed, now, on this side of the veil. What does the scripture say? IF any man be IN Christ, he is THEN a new creation or a new creature!

What does that mean? If I choose to stop at salvation, at the cross, and I believe that death is my transformational key and access so that, after I die, it will give me the ability to transform, to look like Jesus, or a spirit that floats on clouds, I have GRAVELY MISSED IT! If I choose to stop at the STARTING POINT, and not go any further, that is good and okay. I am saved and IF I die a physical death, I will go to heaven. However, if I choose to go INTO and THROUGH the Cross and step into Christ, BY FAITH, out of a desire to pursue in the growing process of my relationship with Him, then I will begin to transform into a new creation, NOW. Why? Because the more time I spend with Him, the more I engage Him, the more I engage Communion ... the more of who He is will multiply IN me and the more of what is IN Him, and in my Father's Kingdom, will become the source of my supply, transforming me from the inside out! In that process, I take on the DNA of Yeshua and His DNA will transform my spirit, change my soul, and transfigure my body. Into what? It will change into the image of Christ in ME, the hope of glory in EVERY AREA in me, in my blood line, my DNA, my house, my children, and all future generations ... my town, my city, my state, my nation, the world, the cosmos, and ALL creation in every realm and dimension!

Remember, we are supposed to go from Glory to Glory, as I mentioned above, and NOT STOP at any one place, any one revelation, any one move of God, or any tradition! Those are supposed to become steppingstones for us to step on them into the "next" that He has for us to step up on, and into.

God is ALWAYS on the move! He ALWAYS brings Revelation of the Mysteries He has ready to unveil for those who choose to step into them. This process will bring about the glory, which will bring about the change He has for us to step into at each level. Each level of glory brings about a change in us. Revelation is always on the move, because it never ceases to reveal the Spirit of Truth. Spirit of Truth will always bring and reveal the multifaceted layers of the TRUTH that is in YHVH, the truth that He wants to show us in order for us to walk in IT and GROW from glory to glory! Which... guess what? It means that the level of revelation I have today about THIS facet of the Truth of YHVH will not be the same tomorrow because the purpose of Truth is to get us to step higher into His glory which, remember, brings transformation and transfiguration!

MATURING OF THE SONS, ANOINTING OF THE KINGS,

AWAKENING THE WARRIORS

Before I begin to break this teaching down, let me just first explain what a Blueprint is. A Blueprint is the original plan, design, and representation of who you were created to be born out of the most intimate place of God, which is His heart, the heart of YHVH, Adonai, our Heavenly Father. This plan that He has for you is incubated and protected in the River of Glory, which is HIS LOVE, which is the essence of who He is, and it FLOWS FROM WITHIN HIS HEART into your spirit man when you engage with it! You see, the fullness of the desires of His heart flow out of His heart through LOVE which is, again, the essence of who He is. This is also known as the River of Gory and, everywhere it goes, it creates the desires that are in His heart!

Let me break it down even more. The most intimate place of YHVH IS HIS HEART, and the very ESSENCE of WHO HE IS… IS LOVE! Love is the most POWERFUL FREQUENCY, ENERGY, AND POWER THAT CREATES! IT CREATES WHAT IS NOT THERE, OR CHANGES WHAT IS THERE … whatever is mutated … INTO THE DESIRE THAT IS IN THE HEART OF ADONAI! The River of Glory, LOVE, is the only power, energy, frequency and light that is the CreaTIVE LIGHT, because it is the only source that can create what is known or seen as creaTED light! That is why LOVE IS THE KEY…relationship is the key that unlocks the portal or gate that is IN and THROUGH the name of YHVH and gives us access in EVERYTHING that is IN HIS NAME! Love is NOT just a feeling and it has nothing to do with "greasy love"! As you just read above, it is the actual energy and power of GOD to create! He does not want us to love Him because He is full of Himself, requiring love from us as a tyrant, NO! He knows, that is THE ONLY KEY that will give us the SAME POWER THAT IS IN HIM! As I have been saying, and will continue to say, ALL of creation IS looking for the sons of God, sons of HIS LIGHT, His LOVE ... to be revealed and put back, bringing forth all that was stolen ... bring His order into all the chaos the enemy brought, in every dimension and timeline ... IN ALL OF CREATION!

I talk more about this in another teaching, "Into Hidden Dimensions and Beyond". I will also be working on another book on that teaching as it is vital for us to understand what the dimensions of YHVH are, and how love is a HUGE NEEDED power that we MUST attain and understand, use, and be responsible for! OK, that was a rabbit trail, however, the Lord wanted me to talk a little bit about love, which IS a foundational principle.

So, your blueprint is WHO YOU ARE truly supposed to BE, and your Destiny Scroll, is WHAT YOU ARE SUPPOSED TO DO. THAT IS TIED INTO WHO YOU ARE ORIGINALLY SUPPOSED TO BE. You can NOT walk out your original Destiny Scroll if you are walking out a mutated blueprint! More on this in a bit.

For example, the blueprint of that which I want to build on this land is a hospital. The destiny (scroll) of this hospital is to be a children's hospital. Now, if all of a sudden someone takes the original blueprint of this building that was supposed to be a hospital and changes it into a casino, then, that building is NO LONGER reflecting the DESTINY it originally had as it is now reflecting a DIFFERENT BLUEPRINT! Do you understand?

So, again, your original blueprint IS in your spirit man, but it is locked up and covered by mutations and chaos as a result of trades done on demonic trading floors. It is, in a sense, asleep and locked up behind the walls of mutation and chaos. This original blueprint locked inside of your spirit man that is dormant IS WAITING FOR SOMETHING TO VIBRATE, BROOD OVER IT, and bring it back alive! It needs the VOICE of Heaven that IS IN your original blueprint, that is IN the Father, to be released over it and WAKE IT UP! How will that happen? By YOU going in the heart of the Father and seeing ... if even just a fragment of your original blueprint! As you are seeing it, be faithful to RELEASE IT ... SPEAKING IT OUT from your position IN Heaven from the heart of Adonai into your spirit man so that heaven can literally overshadow the chaos, and transform it bit by bit into the image of who you are IN the Father!

An arc needs to be formed between the original blueprint that is IN the Father and the Original that He placed IN your spirit man (that is currently dormant under the mutations and chaotic atmosphere that it is imprisoned in) so that what is dormant and imprisoned can COME ALIVE!

That is why we MUST learn how to go to Heaven and release every little part He shows us of our original blueprint into our spirit man, and the atmosphere around us on the earth! Notice, it starts FROM Heaven ... releasing it on the earth. On earth, IN US, as it is IN HEAVEN!

Let's unpack this! Let's look right now at Genesis 15:4 KJV "Then behold, the word of the Lord came to him saying, 'This man will not be your heir, but one who will come forth from your body. He shall be your heir.' And he brought him forth abroad and he said, "look now towards the heavens. Tell the stars if you are able to count them."

You guys, if we leave out our [wrong] western superiority complex and allow God and allow the Word of God, which ARE LIVING BEINGS, like I mentioned before, to teach us and show us truth, we will be shocked at the revelation and the truth that we will see in there; and our transformation process will be much quicker! I am going to say this again just to keep refreshing it in your mind and spirit... the word of God is not black or red words on white paper. The word of God is alive, they are living beings!

Now, how deep do you really want to go in this scripture? Remember, we must leave our western superiority complex aside and read the Bible like a Hebrew in order to see BEYOND the words on the paper...looking through them, into the other dimension of the word and what God wants to show us. Remember, the Greeks teach you how to think and to hear, which is good, but there is more! If you want to stay there and rely on your logic and traditions, that is fine! Again, this has nothing to do with salvation! However, if you want to see beyond what your logic says, and feel the frequency of the Words, to go past the one level of understanding and into one of the facets of the SEVENTY that are in ONE WORD...HOLD ON TO YOUR SEAT, AND LET'S GO!

Listen, even science tells us that at the very core of who we are, at the subatomic level of who we are, we are light! We are beings of pure light that needs to see and feel the frequency of THE LIGHT! Logic is an addition to that, but it is not the end all! Remember, those who understand and communicate, those who worship God, MUST do so IN spirit. What spirit? The Spirit of the pure light of God (aka His spirit) that is IN our spirit man. What else does the word say? "IN spirit" AND "IN Truth", which is The Spirit of Truth that ALWAYS reflects the multi facets of the frequencies of the heart of God.

The Spirit of Truth tells us that we are made in YHVH's image! When we engage THAT frequency of that truth, IT will begin to transform us from a creaTED light being into a creaTIVE light being because, as He IS, so are we IN THIS WORLD, not when we die! Remember what light I said He is? CreaTIVE light! That is what we also MUST BECOME!

1 John 4:16-18 The Passion Translation (TPT)

v16 We have come [not future tense, but we already have come because He made a way for us to go] ... into an intimate experience with God's love, and we TRUST in the love He has for us.

Notice that RELATIONSHIP with Him, aka - to love, obey, to hold Him in affection and to recognize the FULL benefits AND we MUST TRUST IN THAT Love that He is leading us, not a demon, because He gave us the ability to have an INTIMATE EXPERIENCE with His LOVE! Remember, the most intimate place of God IS HIS HEART! When you love Him, you have ACCESS to His heart...which includes the essence of who He is, LOVE, aka the River of Glory, does NOT trick us or allow the enemy to somehow come in and trick us!

Again, what is love? The ultimate power, light, and energy that creates the desire of His heart.

[a] God is love![b] Those who are living IN LOVE ARE LIVING IN God, and God LIVES THROUGH THEM.

Notice, like I said, the most intimate place of God IS His heart. SO, when you are living in the essence of who He is ...love, you are actually living IN God because Love flows out of His heart. Not only are you then living IN God, but He also lives THROUGH YOU! From that place, and IN that place, NO DEMON can come in and trick you! So, do not listen to the LIE of religious spirits who are trying to make you engage with Fear by telling you that somehow you are going to get in trouble because you will be tricked to open yourself up to demons and counterfeit spirits. GRRRR...LIES!!!!

v17 By living IN God [in the most intimate place of God...His heart],[c] love has been brought to its FULL EXPRESSION THROUGH US (What does love do? CREATES what is not there, what is missing, recreates what has been mutated or stolen by the enemy. Notice, we are TO BE the FULL EXPRESSION of the ultimate power and energy that created the desire of the heart of YHVH and out of our innermost being shall flow RIVERS OF LIVING WATER! What river do you think it is talking about? The same River of Glory that flows from the heart of ADONAI, and, everywhere it goes, it births forth HIS desire!) [d]so that we may fearlessly face the day of judgment,[e] because ALL that Jesus NOW IS,[f] so are we IN THIS WORLD. Because now, as He is, so are you, therefore you can do ALL things THROUGH Christ WHO NOW LIVES IN YOU AND YOU IN HIM! There is more to break down in this scripture, but I will do that a bit later.

Now, would you like us to engage His word at the next dimensional level? Well, if you are still reading the book, you definitely want to do that, so let's do it. There are a few things that I want you to see and understand about Abraham, as I will begin to unpack the beginning of his life.

These things are not written down in the Bible, however, they are found in the Hebraic historical accounts as well as in the oral traditions passed down from the priests to the people, in each generation, until they were finally written down.

Really quickly, let's look at who Shem was, so we can get a better understanding of the mentors God sent Abraham in the first part of his life. Shem was one of Noah's sons who God asked to build the city of Salem. The city of Salem became an amazing, holy city that got transdimensionalized into another dimension.

Because Shem was the one that built this city, and this city was a very unique city that was connected to the City of Zion, Shem mentored Abraham, teaching him about the true City of Zion. Shem taught Abraham how to access the City of Zion, showing him the way to it, because we see in the word that it says that Abraham went to a city whose builder and founder is YHVH. Abraham was going in a physical realm but there was a spiritual reality that he was very aware of, because of all that he had learned from both Noah and Shem.

Now, there's not much written in the Bible about Abraham's birth, and there is not a lot of information that we have on it. However, like I stated earlier, it is written down in historical books that Constantine, inspired by the demonic strategy, made sure they were not allowed in the Bible. A whole book could be devoted to this ... and likely has.

All the books that would show or give us a clearer glimpse into our true identity, releasing their frequency into our spirit man, and calling our spirit man forth ... to awaken it out of the spiritual amnesia ... were not allowed in the Bible. All of the books that would reveal "the more" that He gave us, catapulting us into who we really are and all the abilities that we really have through the finished work of the cross, were not allowed. Not only were they not allowed but, if you were caught reading them, you would be imprisoned and even killed! Was this a demonic strategy based on control, manipulation, fear and limitations? ABSOLUTELY. And the sad thing is, that this is STILL operating today! It is YOUR CHOICE if you will continue to engage with it, trading on its nasty floors, OR break the grip and bust out of the prison it has had you in. Some of these books are The Books of Enoch, The Book of Jubilee, The Book of Jasher, The Book of Wars, the Books of Solomon, The Gospel of Thomas, and many more such books. The Gospel of Thomas was a book that IF you were found reading it, you would be immediately put to death!

Rabbit Trail adventure, detour coming up! Before I continue on with this teaching, let's go on a longer rabbit trail that is needed as a foundational understanding for these types of deep teachings. With that in mind, let's just take a look for a bit at The Gospel of Thomas and why was this book such a treat to the evil church systems? The Gospel of Thomas is all about Jesus 'sayings. So, the Gospel of Thomas is not an historical book, a narrative book, but the entire book is literally all the things that Jesus said that we are, we can become, and we are to do. Each verse is called a "saying" because Jesus said it. So, this is what the first saying says... "Whoever reads these truths and understands them, SHALL NEVER DIE!" Do you SEE what Jesus said? If you read and understand the TRUTH of the reality of your identity and all that is connected to that, YOU SHALL NEVER DIE...PHYSICALLY SPEAKING, NOT SPIRITUALLY! Now, let's look at Saying 2 ... "Whoever seeks (choice alert!), let them continue to seek and when they shall find, HE WILL BE DISTURBED. After they will be disturbed, they will be in awe and THEN, they SHALL CONQUER IT ALL!" What do these sayings really mean? Listen, IF YOU CHOOSE TO SEEK, DO NOT STOP.

Keep seeking! Whosoever chooses to seek, they will find! Are you seeking who you really are? If you are looking at your generational line and all you have seen and are see is loss, attack, sickness, death, hopelessness, and lack but, YET, you KNOW something is NOT right ... because not only is that NOT what Jesus said that you are to be, but your spirit man is also crying out that THERE MUST BE MORE ... you are one that NEEDS TO SEEK ... AND KEEP SEEKING! If you are one that sees that your circumstances are contrary to what you KNOW He said you have access to and all that He said you are in and through Him, SEEK AND DON'T STOP SEEKING!

Because, as you keep seeking, YOU WILL FIND the Truth! YOU WILL FIND the answers to your question. Even if you just start getting a glimpse of the truth, it is a start...do NOT stop, but keep seeking! Jesus is trying to encourage those who seek, telling them, "Don't give up, this is NOT who you are supposed to be, for I have made a way FOR MORE! There are mysteries that My Father has hidden for generations, for ages, from man and angels, but NOW, He is revealing them to whosoever chooses to seek them out! He is revealing them to the sons that are allowing themselves to go through the process of maturity, which will give them access to step into the glorification ability that I gave them! DO NOT STOP BUT KEEP SEEKING!" Now, as you find it the Truth, as Truth is beginning to be unfolded and revealed to you in stages, YOU WILL BE DISTURBED! What does He mean?

Listen, as you seek, the Spirit of Revelation and Truth will start unfolding the mysteries of who you really are, your true identity, and IT WILL BE FREAKY! More than likely, you will not have any grid for what you are hearing, seeing, learning! It will be so the opposite of what the religious systems have manipulated you, I believe, through control and fear not only about Him, but about yourself! As that happens, you will feel like you are losing your grip on your identity and the identity of who God is, who Jesus is, and who The Holy Spirit really is! You will be shaken to the core as these truths will shake your false foundation ... as you try to hold on to the identity of your past, based on what you were taught, what you thought you knew and who you thought the Godhead was. You WILL FREAK OUT and you WILL BE DISTURBED, and THAT'S OK!

Let Him shake everything that needs to be shaken ... everything that is a false foundation of your TRUE identity and His TRUE identity, that has been built by the programming of the religious systems through manipulation, fear, and control! Hold on to His experiential love by going IN, seeing yourself IN that love (which is God), TRUSTING THAT LOVE, holding on to that love and RIDE

THAT WAVE INTO YOUR "AWE" MOMENT OF YOUR FREEDOM and INTO YOUR TRUE IDENTITY AND THE ORIGINAL BLUEPRINT!

As you do that, you will SEE clearly that you are not a slave, not a victim, not weak, not bound in chains of limitation, or lack, or fear, or hopelessness, or disease; these things that keep you confined to a chaotic reality. You will no longer agree with this chaotic reality that was built on a platform of control, lies, fear and manipulation; telling you that you must be bound to "carry your cross"! You will no longer agree with this cross of misery, lack, depression, etc., never getting ahead, looking to die, so that you can finally have the victory He promised which can ONLY be attained WHEN YOU DIE! NO!!! Carrying your cross daily is about DAILY remembering that you HAVE died, and are MIRRORING DAILY, your death to the things that LIMIT YOUR TRUE IDENTITY. It is a reminder of ALL the power your TRUE identity, your TRUE original blueprint that He has put in your spirit man! It is a DAILY REMINDER that YOU WERE crucified WITH Christ, died to ALL limitations of your humanity that was bound by the laws of this world and all its chaos that Jesus NAILED AT THE CROSS! It is a DAILY REMINDER that you HAVE BEEN RESURRECTED AND ARE CONTINUALLY being RESURRECTED WITH HIM, living out of THAT reality, IN

THE fullness of RESURRECTION LIFE and RESURRECTION POWER. Yet, you are not even limited to that! It is also a DAILY reminder of the reality that, "NOW, I CAN DO ANYTHING He asks me to do because I CAN DO ALL things ... for, now, I reflect the opposite of ALL that Jesus nailed to the cross and won the victory over, through the cross!" Now, THAT cross IS the cross that He wants me to pick up daily, and follow His lead, because as He IS so am I, NOW, in this world!

In your disturbed state, as you continue to hold on and TRUST His love, you will begin to SEE, HEAR and FEEL that He has given you the ability to do some CRAZY, FREAKY, AMAZINGLY INCREDIBLE STUFF because of the fulness that He has prepared and made ready for whosoever CHOOSES to step THROUGH and into the Covenant of Adoption! You can actually have ALL that Jesus said that He gave us NOW, not when you die! You can be a history maker and a history changer! You are called to be OUTSIDE OF ALL LIMITATIONS of world and all its laws! You CAN walk through walls, walk on water, shift dimensions, manifest matter out of nothing, be in more places at one time, step outside of time, OUTSIDE of all physical laws, any law...AND ENTER HEAVEN ANY TIME YOU DESIRE without death being your entry-point!

Do you guys hear me? If that has never been your grid of understanding, you will be QUITE DISTURBED! Let me break this down a bit more. At first, you will not know if what you are hearing or learning is demonic, witchcraft, new age...your head will spin and fear will try to grab a hold of you because, again, you have NO GRID for all that He is trying to reveal and the religious spirits that have operated through all religious systems, that have and are working hand in hand with the and antichrist spirit, will make sure to keep you in control ... manipulation THROUGH FEAR!

AHHHHH ... but if you KEEP seeking and trusting Him, and you allow the Truth of who you really are to settle in your spirit, YOU WILL BE IN AWE of who you REALLY are IN and THROUGH HIM!

As the "awareness" of the reality of all that you really are settles in your spirit, soul and body ... THEN, YOU SHALL STEP INTO YOUR POSITION of a son, ALLOWING THE SEVEN SPIRITS OF GOD TO MENTOR YOU, transforming you into a mature son, and THEN, being presented back to the Father AS A MATURE SON who will then ANOINT YOU AS A KING, out of your MATURE SONSHIP position and, at THAT POINT, WILL CONQUER IT ALL ... IN and THROUGH YHVH! You WILL conquer it all because as He IS, so are you! ALL authority, power, AND responsibility is also flowing through YOU to conquer it all for His Kingdom!

Gospel of Thomas, Saying 2 ... "Whoever seeks (choice alert!), let them continue to seek and when they shall find, they WILL BE

DISTURBED. After they will be disturbed, they will be in awe, and THEN, they SHALL CONQUER IT ALL!"

Let me speak here to you about the Spirit of Revolution because He has a HUGE part to play in this movement of our awakening! Okay, so for those of you that heard me speak about this, or for those of you who read about this huge encounter I had regarding the Spirit of Revolution, please forgive the repeat. For those of you that have never heard this, let me explain it because it is a must that we understand that it is NO longer about revival, it's about a revolution. I am going to share this powerful encounter I had in Scotland, on Lewis Island, in the Hebrides, where the Lord showed me the season we are in and how the Spirit of Revolution is at the forefront of it.

In August of 2015, the Lord took me to Scotland with a friend of mine on an assignment. On Lewis Island, I had an open vision during a compelling encounter the Lord gave me. I will not put the entire vision and encounter in here, as it is quite long, but you can find it on Kingdom Reflections' website by going to www.kingdomreflections.org. I will briefly mention it because it is essential to us understanding the season we are in, and taking advantage of it, as we will approach the courts of God.

During this encounter, I heard the war cry of William Wallace. I heard the clanging of the swords of the warriors hitting each other as I was continuing to listen to their war cries, but I knew that these particular ones were led by the revolutionist William Wallace. "Daddy, what is this?" Lewis Island is in the Hebrides, and this is the place where the last great revival spread to other nations during the late 1940s and the very beginning of the 1950s.

As I asked the Father to explain why I was hearing what I was hearing, He told me to "look", and I listened to the rumblings of the ancient wells, and I saw its waters come out from under the ground, then onto the ground and, after, lifting upwards, reaching towards the heavens. Then, the Father told me, "It's not about the moves of the past. It's not about revivals of the past, as great as they were for that time and season. These revivals came and died. Though it did bring change to individuals, to churches, and to certain areas, it did not bring a culture change that lasted by bringing a shift in the governments of the world. Even the people that were part of those revivals, as well as some leaders of those great revivals, after a while, they forgot who they were and fell back into spiritual amnesia. However, I am doing a new thing! Watch what I am doing. Look up." As I looked up, I heard such a loud sound, the sound of a torrent coming from Heaven and I saw the heavens open and this powerful torrent of water coming down with such power and loud sound that I actually covered my head with my hands because I thought it was going to crush me. He continued to tell me, "Look up, and I will show you what I am NOW doing and releasing."

As I looked up again, this torrent of water that was coming down met the waters of the ancient well that was coming out of the ground and was reaching upwards, and they connected. As they joined, I saw an explosion of this vast, mighty, torrent of water and the Lord spoke to me and said, "The torrent from Heaven is my Spirit of Revolution that is coming down and connecting with the revival cries of the ones that have gone on before, the ones that are now part of the Cloud of Witnesses. They have also been waiting for this time and season when the Spirit of Revolution will awaken My sons into the knowledge of who they really are, to manifest the fullness of My Kingdom Government...and revolt against the evil and all work and bring not only reformation but reformation releasing a culture change into all the kingdoms... on the earth, under the earth, and in the heavens establishing My kingdoms and My government. At that time, a new revival will cover the earth, like the waters cover the sea. It will be a revival that will be birthed OUT OF A REVOLUTION such as has never happened before. It's not about revival it's about a REVOLUTION that has been released led by the Spirit of Revolution, and you guys, like him or not, He said, all the way back in 2015, [now President] Donald Trump IS part of this revolution.

I did not find out until much later that President Trump's mother, Mary Ann Smith MacLeod, comes from Lewis Island ... right where I was standing ... and that his two great aunts were part of this revival 1949-1952.

Man, oh man, little did I understand at that time, what a HUGE mandate President Trump had and has, regarding the release of the Spirit of Revolution. Little did I know or understand how President Trump's original blueprint carries the "DNA" of the Father's heart, that He placed IN the Spirit of Revolution that has been released in August of 2015! Since then, President Trump has taken his position with Spirit of Revolution, along with ALL of Heaven, all the beings God has created and the Sons of Liberty that have CHOSEN to hear and STEP INTO this call and fight! President Trump is FIGHTING like no other president of any nation, in all of history of humanity, against the putrid, malevolent, beyond evil, reptilian, demonic, satanic, luciferic, black hat, cabalistic agenda, the shadow government, … that has been in full operation for thousands of years in EVERY government on the face of earth! The fight is on against all this unbelievable evil ON behalf of ALL the children in the entire world that have been fed upon, tortured alive, raped even as newborn babies, their blood used as the highest form of drug for power, life, youth, experiments and other HORRORS! WE ARE IN A COSMIC WAR and President Trump, from being in his position with Christ IN the Father, is leading this war. Are you called to also join the ranks of being one of the Sons of Liberty that is helping annihilate THE BIGGEST, DARKEST, MOST EVIL TRADING FLOOR IN THE HISTORY OF HUMANITY, THAT IS BUILT ON THE BLOOD, FLESH, DESTINIES AND BLUEPRINTS OF THE BABIES AND CHILDREN?

You guys, HERE is TRULY a man that KNOWS and FULLY lives completely OUT OF HIS ORIGINAL blueprint, STANDING IN his mountain, FIRMLY standing IN his God given identity … his original blueprint! I honor him and his family for the CHOICE he made to walk out his original blueprint which…I know most of you know the weightiness of it. He sure as heck did not have to, BUT he heard the call and did not turn back! DO YOU HEAR THE CALL? Again, YOUR CHOICE CHOOSES YOU!

Now, let's get back and finish my point about Constantine being used by the enemy to try and control our understanding of our identity by deciding what books would be allowed in the Bible and what books he was determined to leave out. By doing so, Constantine, and the powers that be, were able to take full control of every aspect of the society, the people, and the church. He made agreements with the head of the religious systems to crush the true identity and anyone daring to search that truth, through control, manipulation, fear and death. RELIGION IS EVIL and God HATES IT! He wants RELATIONSHIP! This is STILL alive and very much in power, today as well!

Unfortunately, these demonic strategies have worked thus far because we have believed the lies of the enemy, the devil, BASED IN FEAR, and we have made a covenant with death, giving these demons, evil rulers, principalities and powers legal right to keep us bound in the limitations and a chaotic reality that is a mutated identity!

Most of us have agreed with their lies and, not only that, we have echoed out these lies by coming into agreement with them and trading on all of these demonic trading floors! "Well, I can't do that. I will never do that. I am not special. Only special ones can do that! The only time I will see Jesus and the Father is when I die. Oh, I can't talk to angels, or other beings, I can't talk to my cloud of witnesses because that is talking to dead, that is evil! I can't do that, go there, say this because then I open myself up to a demon or because they will trick me! Oh, I have to be careful because so and so says this is witchcraft and new age and I am walking in deception and an angel of light will come in and trick me! I am a wicked man/woman, I am but a sinner saved by grace that has to carry his/her cross and crawl till I finally go to Heaven where I will finally walk-in victory. I am but a slave in my father's house; I am but His bond servant. I am not like God, that is heresy!" Oh my gosh! Do you see? Lies, lies! Do you see the programming that has been done in us? However, once YOU SEE YOUR ORIGINAL BLUEPRINT, the programing will dissipate!

You see, if we do not know who we are, our TRUE identity, we will NEVER walk in His full ability given to us. We will never walk in our authority, power, and responsibility because, again, we agree with the lying demons spewing lies that are rooted IN FEAR, working with the

Antichrist Spirit, denying who we are, denying us ENTRY into the fulness of all that our Father gave us! As I mentioned above, there is a gospel that is being preached, but it denies His power IN US! "That is demonic. That's witchcraft. No one can just go to Heaven! You can't REALLY do all that Jesus did! That was for back then, and only He and His disciples could do that. Yeah, He did all that but, if you think you can do it, you are falling in deception! Thinking you can trans-relocate or walk-through walls or create substance out of nothing is HERESY... it is witchcraft! Stay away from that deception!" Break OUT of that programming and come out of agreement with those principalities and powers! You have a choice! This is what you will learn to do, in this book. I am so excited for you to do just that!

Do you know how God must feel when we come in agreement with these lying demons negating the totality of all that He did in order give us FULL access BACK into all that Adam lost, into all that lucifer traded? Can you even comprehend or imagine how Yeshuah feels when every time someone talks about the supernatural power of God, the supernatural power of Jesus, and all the abilities that He gave us, immediately, there are those that give all credit of THIS power to the devil, witches, and demons by saying "That's evil ... that's witchcraft!" Wait, WAIT...hold up!!!! SO, are we to agree with the "thought" that God is weak, or that He is no longer capable of doing supernatural, superhuman interventions THROUGH US, as HIS children?

He gave us all these abilities through the massive sacrifice, the ULTIMATE TRADE, of His first, begotten son, Yeshuah and now, we are giving credit to the devil, to witches, and demons saying that when you see such power, or manifesting such power, it is them doing it? Oh, my goodness!!!! Do you see how these principalities are trying to DENY the power of CHRIST IN ME, the hope of glory, and crediting ALL powers to the kingdom in darkness? So sad how, throughout centuries, we have been giving credit to the devil and denying the full power of YHVH operating IN and through us! Because of this, hundreds of thousands of men, and ESPECIALLY women, were burned at the stake, beheaded, ripped and pulled apart by tortured mechanisms in horrific ways IN the name of God, Jesus, and Christianity, throughout the ages, and many of these that were tortured were only operating out of their original blueprint!

You and I have a HUGE job to do because ALL of creation is groaning and looking to US to bring back YHVH's kingdom – government order. If the enemy can keep us lethargic, asleep, IN FEAR, manipulation and control THROUGH FEAR ... in its prison as weak slaves, he has won the battle!

Listen, you can go to Heaven when you die (if that is what you believe). You can go limping, weak, sick, always feeling defeated, full of bruises, always feeling like you are getting your bootie kicked, licking your wounds AND, because you gave your life to Jesus at the cross, you are STILL going to Heaven when you die! Remember, I said if salvation is where you choose to stop, it's okay. OR you can choose to walk, NOW, as a king that is birthed out of sonship from your position IN Heaven! From THAT position, releasing the power, authority, and responsibility of His kingdom government in you, in your family, in your neighborhood, in your community, in your city, in your nation, on the earth, and in all of creation. Why? Because you chose to not just stop at the cross, at salvation but you chose to go THROUGH THE CROSS, into resurrection life and resurrection power now, not when you die! What does this mean? The FULL power that Jesus used to manifest the Kingdom of the Father when He walked on earth, you can also manifest. The FULL power that rose Him from the grave into resurrection life and resurrection power, at which point our enemy, death, was also defeated, will and CAN manifest in you! You have CHOSEN to go through the cross into it ALL because Jesus made a way for you and you recognize it, and you are choosing to be chosen!

Remember me mentioning at the beginning (and have are referenced it often) the scripture that states that many are called, but few are chosen? Again, that does not mean that God sits up there looking at us saying, "hmm.... I choose you, and you, not you ... and I choose you, and I skip you ... You are much prettier, and you are stronger, so I choose you." NO! The reason few are chosen is that FEW CHOOSE TO BE CHOSEN BECAUSE FEW CHOOSE TO

DO THE WORK! OUR CHOICE CHOOSES US! He already WON the victory for us as He became the ultimate trade! Now, we have to CHOOSE to pick up the tools, the abilities He gave us, the authority and power He won for us, the keys He gave us, the weapons and army He gave us and USE it to establish His finished work!

Again, before we get off this rabbit trail, though much needed, IT IS NO LONGER ABOUT REVIVAL, BUT ABOUT A REVOLUTION! Listen, you only need to revive someone who is DEAD! Seriously, how many more centuries will the Lord have to revive His sons? "Revived...YAY!!! Oh, sorry dead again. REVIVED...YEAY!!! Ohhh, sorry... dead again!! Let's pray again for revival! Let's have, again, revival meeting and conferences because year after year after year, we keep dying!" Seriously!!!??!! He is looking for the warriors, the sons, the kings that have allowed the Spirit of Revolution to hit them and they are REVOLTING against all the lies of the enemy. They are TAKING IT ALL BACK BY FORCE AND THEY WILL LOOK AT THE CROSS THEY ARE CARRYING, AS A REMINDER THAT THEY ARE GONNA LIVE IN AND THROUGH THE RESURRECTION LIFE ... NO LONGER DYING! God needs the Sons, Kings, Warriors, Knights to STAY IN resurrection LIFE at all times and operate OUT OF resurrection POWER! HALLELUJAH! Off the rabbit trail for now.

Now, to get back to Abraham. I left off discussing how Sham was teaching Abraham about the true City of Zion, and though Abraham was going into a physical realm, there was a spiritual reality that he became very aware of. Now, Abraham lived with Sham and Noah for 39 years. More on this in a bit.

So, we know he met his wife Sarah, and, for a long time, they could not have any children. Abraham thought he had a brilliant idea that he needed to help God, and he got Haggai pregnant!

So, The Lord tells Abraham that the son that is coming "out of your loins, he shall be your heir". Now, did Ishmael not come out of Abraham's loins? He did, however, God was talking about a seed line. He was talking about the DNA because something was not right with that DNA. Remember the devil is always after DNA, after the seed line, the bloodline so that he can steal the inheritance and manifest himself through it, bringing the counterfeit, bringing a mutated version of the blueprint of God.

The enemy is always wanting to bring something to birth before its season, to birth. The counterfeit, to bring destruction and chaos to the authentic birthing of the purposes and the desire of God in your life. We must remember that the enemy cannot create anything! He is a thief, so he steals, mutates and counterfeits.

This is why the Father wants to teach us about Trading Floors, so we can know what they are, and for us to start to get off of them. He is also teaching us about our original blueprint, so that we can begin to walk THAT, no longer walking the counterfeit one and, as we do that, we will be walking our original Destiny Scrolls!

This is very important for us to always keep in mind. The Kingdom of Heaven will not come upon anything that does not look like it. Therefore, if we are not walking with the authentic, original blueprint of God that He intertwined inside of our spirit man, we will never be able to walk out our original Destiny Scrolls. This is because He is ALWAYS LOOKING FOR A SHADOW of Himself ... "on earth as it is in heaven". If He does not see that shadow here on the earth, here in you and me, He will never allow what is pure, original, and of Himself to come upon it. He will not allow it to come upon something that is NOT of Him.

Remember, Peter's SHADOW healed the sick! Why??? Because God saw a shadow of Himself in and through Peter and the Kingdom of Heaven come upon what was of Himself, and healing was released! Do you understand? More on this in a bit.

What ends up happening is that, because we don't really know who we are, and we are not walking in our original blueprint (therefore, NOT walking in our original Destiny Scrolls) we then want to copy somebody else's, blueprint because we do not know who we are! "Hmm...maybe I can be a prophet also like so and so ... or hmm, I have been a worship leader, but I really think I can also be a pastor like them! I want to try to do what they do!" So, there comes competition and jealousy. Therefore, in essence, we are walking with SPIRITUAL AMNESIA, always wanting to be someone and do something that we see the other person doing! However, with this book, you are learning how to engage YOUR original blueprint, so that you can start becoming who YOU really were created to be and start walking out each phase of your original Destiny Scrolls.

OUTSIDE OF TIME AND SPACE

METAMORPHOSIS

We have to take a look at Nimrod, as he has a huge part in this story. Who was Nimrod? Nimrod was the son of Cush, who was the son of Ham, who was the son of Noah. Oh, something really funky was going on with that seed line of Ham! It was very mutated and polluted, but that is for another book.

So, let's look a little bit deeper at Nimrod by looking at Genesis 10:8. I want you guys to see something very powerful here in this verse. I know we have read this before, but I bet a lot of us have not noticed something very interesting happening to Nimrod according to this verse. "And Cush begat Nimrod and he BEGAN TO BECOME a mighty one (a *giant*) IN THE EARTH." Now, if we break this scripture down, we see that something very peculiar happened to Nimrod. We can look at three things that the scriptures show that took place with him. First, the scripture says that he "began to be". In Hebrew, this is chalal, which means "to become profaned, defiled, polluted, ritually, sexually, genetically on a DNA level".

The second thing that we see from this verse that happened to Nimrod is what he began to change genetically "into". It says that "he began to change genetically into a M IGHTY ONE. In Hebrew, this means a "GIBOR", meaning a giant, a mighty one, a man of old, Nephilim. GIBOR is singular, speaking of one. This word, Giborim (plural of Gibor) is the same word used in the Bible. In Genesis 6:4, when it talks about the sons of God coming and impregnating the daughters of man. Their children were GIBORIM/giant ones, again, also known as Nephilim. They are also seen to be kin to the Greek Titans, being of enormous size.

SO, the second thing that we see CLEAR in this short verse is that Nimrod began to CHANGE GENETICALLY, ON A DNA LEVEL, profaned, defiled or polluted, THROUGH agreements he made ... either through sexual ritual or other rituals.

The third thing we see in the scripture that is so interesting is that Nimrod BEGAN TO CHANGE GENETICALLY, ON A DNA LEVEL, INTO A NEW CREATURE ... A GIANT, WHILE ON THE EARTH!!!

We see that something happened to Nimrod's DNA/bloodline as it says that "he began to be a gibor", meaning that something turned on in him, like a switch in his DNA, as a result of his decisions, triggering a CHANGE in him, FROM ONE TYPE OF BEING INTO ANOTHER!

Wow! Come on! DO YOU SEE THAT???! Okay, so, with this in mind, let's go visit the scripture that I mentioned at the beginning:
2 Corinthians 5:17 Therefore, IF anyone is IN Christ (notice that we have a CHOICE as I stated a few times above), then, he IS a NEW CREATION, or new creature, AND OLD things, [including our mutated and polluted DNA and the genetic triggers], HAVE PASSED AWAY; behold, ALL THINGS [from the inside ... out ... starting with the spirit being awakened, bringing change and transformation to the soul, recreating the DNA, the blood line and seed line which in turn brings transfiguration to the body] HAVE become NEW!

So, let's see now what The Lord is trying to show us here? LISTEN, if this guy called Nimrod, because of a CHOICE that he made, was able to change his DNA while on earth, transforming his DNA from one state into another, and transfiguring his body, from one creature or creation into another, HOW MUCH MORE SHOULD WE BE ABLE TO DO JUST THAT, AND

MORE, BECAUSE OF THE BLOOD AND BODY OF YESHUA, BECAUSE OF THE CROSS, BECAUSE OF THE COVENANT OF ADOPTION, AND EVERYTHING HE GAVE US?

Let me please make this point again... Guys, God doesn't need us to change into "a new creation" when we die! There is no war past the Pearly Gates! The war is NOW, here, in the Kingdom of the Earth and in ALL of creation! Therefore, He needs us to KNOW who we REALLY are, so that we can start to change, become transformed on the inside, and transfigured on the outside! As we do that, we become those "sons of God", aka...sons of light...creaTIVE light, that all of creation is groaning for to bring back YHVH's order in all realms, dimensions, and timelines! You guys, WE HAVE A BIG JOB TO DO!

This war is NOT REALLY the angel's job to fight. They were created to come alongside of US as our MIGHTY, POWERFUL, [NO JOKE] BUTT KICKING WARRIORS, OUR GREAT HELP! This, however, only happens when WE get up in our position and do the job of OUR FATHER as mature sons, anointed as kings and appointed as priests under the Order of Melchezadacha! Do you understand? They're doing some of our job UNTIL we AWAKEN out of our spiritual amnesia and REVOLT against all the lies of the enemy and get our buttocks UP ... IN OUR POSITION of power, authority AND RESPONSIBILITY!

Back to Nimrod. Now, as Nimrod started to change, we see that not only did his DNA completely change but, because his DNA changed, during that change, it turned on triggers in his ability to see beyond the realm of his natural sight and he began to see, and get insight, knowledge, and understanding that he did not have before. With these new abilities, he began to SEE and KNOW the location of where to build his city Shinar (Babilonia). Not only that but, more in particular, he began to know where to build The Tower of Babel, that would be EXACTLY UNDER A DIMENSION GATE to where EloHim was. We know this because we see Elohim saying," Let us go down and confuse their tongues because, if not, they will achieve to do what they proposed to do in their heart."

Here is the difference. God showed Shem where to build the City of Salem, out of the relationship Shem had with YHVH, and Nimrod knew that Shem's city had a gate, a portal into the City of Zion, the City of God, where Shem was able to go in and out. Nimrod wanted to copy the same thing! However, instead of receiving that revelation out of relationship with YHVH, Nimrod received it out of a demonic revelation, when he engaged with the ritual that brought forth the change in his DNA. When your DNA changes, you have inside that which you never had before!

Ohh, how I feel the presence of the Lord as I am typing this out! Father, I come into agreement with all that You are doing in, for, and through each person that is reading this book! Let these words in this book, and the frequency that they carry, the frequency of the Spirit of Truth, Spirit of Revelation, and Mystery, intertwine inside their spirit man, and awaken them into the reality of who they really are! Allow the words of this book and the frequency and reflections they carry to bring the transformation that you have for, not only them, but for their entire bloodline! May this start with them, as they engage YOUR WORDS ... THE LIVING LETTERS and their original blueprint!! Let the Spirit of Faith arise from within the depths of their spirit and bring forth the DESIRE FOR CHANGE!

I see the Cloud of Witnesses swirling as a multicolored, almost translucent, cloud over the ones who are reading this book. Do you understand that YOUR Cloud of Witnesses are coming INTO agreement with all that you will be doing, learning and engaging out of this revelation YHVH released! They are excited that you ARE LEARNING and picking up where they have left off! They are HERE, ready to come alongside you! THE HOSTS OF HEAVEN THAT YHVH HAS ASSIGNED TO YOU, AND TO YOUR BLOODLINE, ARE ALSO PRESENT! THIS IS AN APPOINTED TIME, YOUR APPOINTED TIME OF ENGAGEMENT, WITH ALL WHO ARE PART OF YOUR ORIGINAL BLUEPRINT! I will discuss all that are connected to your original blueprint, in a later chapter.

Take a few moments to engage with what I am saying, with what you are reading and WRITE DOWN what you may SENSE, FEEL, SEE, SMELL AND HEAR. DO NOT, NOT, NOT DISCOUNT ANYTHING! First thing you think, or you sense, or see, or feel, or smell, or hear, write it down and ENGAGE IT! Whatever that is...be faithful in the small and the increase comes.

The City of Salem was a real city on the earth, but it was also an entry point into another dimension. It had access to go into the City of Zion, because it became known as a city of refuge for those who found it. I will try to draw this picture for you with words, without you being able to see my hands. Everything with the Lord is overlapping. Each "dimension" has an entry point of a gate into another dimension, if you will. As you read the following verse, imagine my hands raising one above the other as though this plateau and then this other plateau ... and this next plateau, each going higher.

If we look in Psalm 76:1-2, I want you to watch. 1b..." His name is great in Israel. 2. His tabernacle [in Hebrew, this is His sanctuary, His tent, His covert, His lair and thicket] is IN Salem and His dwelling place [habitation, home], IS IN Zion." Do you see the overlapping dimensions that have gates that gives "whosoever chooses" access to go into the next?

You are a spirit who has a soul who lives in a body. Do you understand? You're supposed to open up those gates to let what is on the inside of your SPIRIT to flow into the gates of your soul and out through the gates of your body. Overlapping dimensions.

The kingdom of the earth is here all around us. The Kingdom of God is in your spirit man, and the Kingdom of Heaven is here at hand ... it is as close to you as the air that you breathe! Here, put your hand directly (close) in front of your face and breathe. Do you feel that breath? That is how close the Kingdom of Heaven is! That is what it means "at hand". It is as close to you as the air that you breathe. ALL YOU NEED TO DO IS CHOOSE TO STEP INTO IT BY FAITH!

Do you see how it is all about overlapping dimensions that give you access, BECAUSE OF THE CROSS, to go through these gates into the other dimensions of YHVH? Remember the Scripture says in Psalm 24:9 (TPT): "So wake up, YOU LIVING GATEWAYS, and rejoice! Fling wide your ageless doors of destiny! Here He comes, the

King of Glory is ready to come in." In the Aramaic Bible in Plain English … "Lift up your heads, oh, Gates; be lifted up, oh gates of eternity, that the King of Glory may enter!"

Who do you think those gates are? Did you know that Russian geneticists discovered that the human DNA IS A PORTAL…a gateway? They took human DNA and put it in a special vacuum, and they started the vacuum at very high speeds, and they realized, as the DNA spun at that speed, there was actually a gate that opened up inside that molecule of the human DNA! So, again, who do you think those gates are? It is you and me!

Now, I also want you to notice something else hugely important in this verse. Do you remember when I said that numbers are huge, and that the Lord speaks through numbers? Also, do you remember what He is trying to unveil to us when we see a pattern of TWO in the word? Two speaks of two points meeting, agreeing, and, as they do, it opens up a widow in heaven and it poured down whatsoever the agreement, aka the "ARC", that was formed was about! Now, do you also remember what I said a bit earlier that God IS LOOKING FOR A SHADOW OF HIMSELF, on the earth, so that He can come and fill it?

"On earth AS IT IS IN HEAVEN" … So, look at this wonderful mystery that He is unveiling yet again in this scripture IF we CHOOSE to OPEN UP OUR GATES … to "WAKE UP" … to "lift up our heads" IN ACKNOWLEDGMENT of who WE ARE. In this scripture, He wants us to acknowledge that we are gates/portals! Why must we choose to "lift up our heads", to "wake up" as living gates? Because He is looking for someone who chooses to open up their gates so that His light could flow through us, becoming His SHADOW, HIS REFLECTION, on earth as He is in heaven! This happens as "those that are in the SECRET PLACE [the most INTIMATE PLACE OF GOD … which IS HIS HEART] OF THE MOST HIGH, SHALL (they will THEN) abide under the SHADOW of His wing."

How is a shadow created? You MUST be in the presence of a GREATER LIGHT. Remember what light is inside His heart? CreaTIVE light, which is LOVE, because LOVE is the essence of WHO HE IS, that flows out of Him as the River of Glory. As you absorb THAT light, you then become a SHADOW OF THAT LIGHT and THEN, A REFLECTION of Him!

As you become a reflection of that light, you will do ALL THAT HE DOES because you CAN NOW DO ALL THINGS THROUGH CHRIST! WOW!!!

So, again, as we go in that secret place, IN HIS HEART, and we ABSORB that greater light in us, becoming a shadow of Him, there is a RAPID RESPONSE … a "flinging wide" of the ETERNAL GATES, OR THE AGELESS DOORS OF DESTINY … WHOSE DESTINY???? YOURS AND MINE! Not only your destiny but the destiny of your entire bloodline! It is, again, YOUR CHOICE to, 1…Go into that secret place, His heart and 2…Absorb THAT creatiVE light, His love, in you 3…becoming a shadow of Him on the earth, 4…so that, at that point, you can become the literal reflection of all that He is and ALL that He has. This was WHO YOU WERE CREATED TO BE FROM BEFORE THE FOUNDATIONS OF THE WORLD, FROM ETERNITY, AND FROM AN AGELESS TIME!

Let me continue to break it down even more. At that point when you choose to be His Gate, and the rapid response come from the ageless and eternal gates that holds YOUR destiny, your original blueprint, an ARC IS FORMED BETWEEN YOU AS THE GATE AND THE ETERNAL GATE that holds your original blueprint. As you, the gate, AND the ancient, eternal, ageless gate connect, IN AGREEMENT (like saying, "HEY, I HEAR THE FREQUENCY OF ADONAI, EL ELYON COME THROUGH YOUR GATE! I RECOGNIZE THAT! I HAVE BEEN WAITING FOR YOU TO RELEASE THE FREQUENCY OF WHO YOU ARE IN AND THROUGH HIM … becoming His shadow, so that I CAN COME INTO AGREEMENT WITH THAT TESTIMONY that Adonai

HAS entrusted me to hold and keep, for such a time as this!") an arc is created.

Now, this ARC that is/was created is an agreement. It is formed and what is the result? Watch this... (again, Psalms 24:7-10): "Here He COMES [not will come]. The King of Glory IS READY to come IN. He is the Lord of Victory armed and ready for battle [WOOHOO!!!]. Mighty one, the invincible commander of heaven's hosts!" THAT IS WHO COMES IN AND THROUGH YOU, not only for you, but for your entire bloodline, seed-line, because in or behind the eternal, ageless doors of your destiny that holds your original blueprint, He has ALREADY WON IT ALL...for you! YOU ARE NOW, just becoming a REFLECTION OF THAT FINAL ACT, that NOW flows THROUGH YOUR GATES, on earth, under the earth and in all of creation.

Remember, everything with The Lord is about becoming a shadow, mirroring, reflecting, and overlapping to give you and I access into the next. There was a Tabernacle IN Heaven and Moses built a tabernacle on earth, as a reflection of the one in Heaven. That earthly one had a portal, in the Holy of Holies, to bring the High Priests from the earthly Holy of Holies INTO the habitation of Ha'Shem!

Where do you think the Ark of Covenant is now? It is IN YOU AND ME! WE ARE THE CARRIERS OF HIS PROMISES, carriers of His inheritance, so that ALL of creation can benefit as we BECOME THE GATES and portals. WHY? It is so that we can release THAT original blueprint for and into all of creation, ARCING [come into agreement with] ALL THAT HE HAS KEPT BEHIND the Ageless, Eternal gates of Destiny!

If we operate out of THAT, do you understand that, at THAT point, ALL OF CREATION WILL WALK OUT AND DISPLAY THEIR AGELESS, ETERNAL DESTINY... their original blueprint, in every dimension, every realm and every timeline, BECAUSE WE CHOOSE TO STEP IN OUR POSITION AND WALK OUT OUR BLUEPRINT!

I feel the presence of The Lord so very strong, even as I type these lines above. I encourage you to stop right now if you are also sensing or feeling HIS presence and engage with Him through your desire. Just let the desire that you have for Him (see, feel, or sense Him) to engage all these truths that He is unveiling to you and draw you into Him. Just say, "Father, I desire to engage in Your presence ... I think, I sense, or feel You, Your presence, and your angelic hosts. I feel these words that I have read reverberate in my spirit and I desire to engage them ... to engage You! By faith, I allow the eyes of my imagination to paint the desire I have for you." Now, stay there and ALLOW your desire of what you want to see of HIM show you through your God given imagination. Write down what you sense, hear, feel, see, smell. Do not discount anything!

It is your choice, and my choice, how deep He will take us. Do you choose to engage, no matter how little you THINK you see or sense ... or do you get frustrated, giving up, allowing the enemy to lie to you that you cannot see or feel anything?

THE VOICE OF THE CELESTIAL

Everything in creation has a voice. Nothing is inanimate. Everything IS alive and everything has a voice. Everything that the Father has created IS PART OF YOUR INHERITANCE! "Everything" means EVERYTHING on the earth and in the heavens, in every dimension. EVERYTHING is every thing that God made, everything seen and unseen on the earth, under the earth, in the cosmos, in the multiverses. He created it ALL, as part of OUR INHERITANCE as His mature sons! So, ALL OF "THAT" is looking to us, crying out for us, the sons of God, to be revealed and for us to take our position of authority, power, and responsibility to bring back YHVH's Kingdom Government in their world!

Remember that the scripture tells us that if we are found faithful in the small and overcome, He will make us rulers over cities, nations. That is not referring to cities here on the earth, or the nations of the earth...there would not be enough! He is referring to worlds! "In My Father's house (his abode, His realms and dimensions) there are MANY MANSIONS (worlds filled with riches) and I go to PREPARE a place for YOU!" He HAS already prepared that place of VICTORY for us THROUGH the cross. Now all we need to do is TAKE OUR RIGHTFUL POSITION AND RULE!

Now, I want you to see something else that is so incredible. Our universe, JUST IN THE LITTLE CORNER OF IT THAT THEY CAN SEE, they have seen over 200 BILLION to a suggested TWO TRILLION OR MORE GALAXIES! Each galaxy has over 100 BILLION stars or more in it; more than there are the grains of sand on earth! Please don't rush reading these words and numbers, but stop and take this in.

You know, when you look at an image from Nasa of all these little dots of light in space, and you see a gazillion of them? Well, those are GALAXIES and each of those little dots of light, have hundreds of

BILLION stars in it! Each year, they discovered NEW planets OUTSIDE OUR MILKY WAY! So far, they have discovered 4,000 planets, worlds BEYOND our solar system!

There are TRILLIONS of other planets in OUR galaxy, which itself is one of the HUNDREDS OF BILLIONS of galaxies in the SEEN universe. Also, on November 4, 2013, astronomers reported that, based on Kepler data, there could be as many as 40 BILLION earth-size planets orbiting the habitable zone called the Goldilocks zone. Again, this is JUST in the little corner of our universe that they can see! They are now also thinking and theorizing that there may be multiverses not just our universe with parallel universes! OMGOSH! And they also have noticed that the universe keeps expanding! Do you know why? Because God loves to create, and he keeps creating! Do you know why He keeps creating? Because he KEEPS ADDING ON TO YOUR INHERITANCE! HE NEVER STOPS ADDING ON TO YOUR AND MY INHERITANCE! ALLLLLL OF THAT, IS LOOKING FOR YOU TO AWAKEN, MATURE, BE ANOINTED AS A KING OUT OF YOUR POSITION AS A MATURE SON, AND BE APPOINTED AS A PRIEST UNDER THE ORDER OF MELCHIZEDEK TO RESTORE, CO-RULE, AND CO-CREATE WITH YOUR DADDY!

I want you to understand something so powerful! You see, God fashioned you when His heart's desire SPOKE YOU INTO HIM, before He created anything else, and braided your spirit man with certain facets of His DNA which are IN your original blueprint. Now, when He started to create the rest, the same frequency or facets of who He is THAT HE PUT IN YOU, He ALSO put in different planets and stars that are out there ... because THOSE ARE PART OF YOUR INHERITANCE ... HE MADE THEM FOR YOU! Therefore, certain stars, planets, and galaxies belong to you, and certain others belong to another person and other galaxies, AKA MANSIONS, belong to another person. Therefore, everything He created IS in our inheritance!

Remember what I said that cosmologists have realized that the Universe KEEPS EXPANDING because God KEEPS CREATING! SO, He is STILL ADDING TO YOUR INHERITANCE!

So, ALL OF THAT is groaning for YOU and me to AWAKEN, START TO OPERATE OUT OF OUR ORIGINAL BLUEPRINT, and to bring back the order of YHVH in all the chaos that lucifer did. Why? Because that IS YOUR INHERITANCE and since the enemy cannot have inheritance, he goes after ours ... INCLUDING ALL THAT IS IN THE COSMOS, SEEN AND UNSEEN! Again, I say, we are HUGE IN and THROUGH HIM, and we have a BIG job to do.

Listen, DNA HAS a sound, a song! I will not go too deep about it in this book, however in the Unveiling the Mysteries of Communion I do go much deeper in this subject. Here I will just mention it because I want you guys to really start to understand who you REALLY ARE! So, DNA has a song and also has colors. We see in Psalm 139:15, 15 My frame was not hidden from You, When I was being formed in the secret place (remember me discussing what that secret place is? The most intimate place of God...HIS HEART) ... And intricately and skillfully formed (as if embroidered with MANY COLORS) [as if wrought with a needle] in the depths or lowest parts of the earth.

EARTH here does not mean our earth, but it is a word used to describe the unseen world, a world as remote from human eyes as the depths of the earth. HOWEVER, GUESS WHAT WE ARE LEARNING???? That it is NOT UNSEEN to whosoever chooses to be in that secret place from where, all things are visible. In Hebrew, the word Eretz is used which refers to the promised land. Is our promised land ON THE EARTH? NOT MINE! Where is our Promise Land?

So then, we were formed in His heart, birthed out of His desire, flowing out of LOVE, which is the most powerful energy and light that creates, also known as The River of Glory! We were embroidered as with a needle with many colors. Color carries frequencies, sounds! This is when He put the facets of who He is, that must shine through us, the colors of His DNA, IN our DNA, weaving us together! He did this IN THE PROMISED LAND, NOT on the earth! Remember He formed us BEFORE the FOUNDATIONS OF THE WORLDS or during a time before anything was created!

Now let's look at the stars for a minute or more...

The stars ALSO have a sound and song! Each planet and star have individual sounds or songs! The ones that are part of your inheritance carry the FREQUENCY THAT YOU CARRY...the frequency that YHVH put inside your original blueprint, your original DNA!

Let me make this point here...Stars are stars and angels are angels! The root word in Aramaic for angel is Malak. The root word for stars in Aramaic is kochav.

Now let's look at this scripture from Psalm 119:1-4 and what it says: v1." The heavens declare the glory of God and the sky/firmament (which includes all that is there...all the stars, planets) PROCLAIM (which means to speak out for all to hear, a declaration) THE WORKS OF HIS HANDS."

What is the biggest, most important and powerful work of His hands? YOU, ME, and our inheritance which IS CALLING OUT, groaning, for US to awaken! They are calling forth a proclamation saying, "Wake up, awaken you warrior into the reality of who you are! We are all waiting on you, to step UP, manifesting your original blueprint and walk out your original destiny scroll because we need you! You are not a slave, a weak human being bound by the limitations of the laws of chaos and death...you ARE A SPIRIT BEING! You have access to step NOW with Christ, into the Creator, who is your Father and AWAKEN OUT OF YOUR SPIRITUAL AMNESIA! RISE UP, OH, SON OF LIGHT, WARRIOR OF LIGHT AND TAKE YOUR RIGHTFUL POSITION AND BRING BACK HIS KINGDOM GOVERNMENT AND HIS ORDER!"

v2. Day after day they pour out speech and night after night, they communicate KNOWLEDGE. (What knowledge? The knowledge of

WHO WE REALLY ARE! The knowledge of the Divine plan of God that was once hidden from humans and angels, but NOW, God is revealing it to the spiritually mature ones who are READY for understanding!)

Do you understand that NIGHT AFTER NIGHT, this means year after year, decade after decade, century after century, and generation after generation they have been communicating KNOWLEDGE TO THE SPIRIT MAN OF EVERYONE IN YOUR GENERATIONAL LINE HOPING THAT SOMEONE IN IT WILL HEAR THEM TRYING TO COMMUNICATE THIS KNOWLEDGE!

This means that from the beginning of lucifer's thievery and trading on OUR inheritance, after JESUS MADE A WAY FOR YOU AND ME TO GET IT ALL BACK by given us access to go THROUGH THE CROSS... they (THE HEAVENS, THE FIRMAMENTS AND ALL THAT IS IN THERE) HAVE BEEN SPEAKING THIS KNOWLEDGE HOPING THAT, NOW, YOU, THE ONE READING THIS, OR THE ONE LEARNING ABOUT THESE THINGS, CAN HEAR THEM! They ALWAYS release and reflect the desire of Adonai, your original blueprint, reminding you of who you are, pointing you ALWAYS back to Him, so that you can awaken!

Let's go to verse three.
v3.   There are no words where their VOICE is NOT heard.

What does this mean? They do not have words like you and I have. HOWEVER, they carry the VOICE of the frequency of GOD. As they release THAT, there is NO PLACE on earth, UNDER the earth, and in ALL of creation that their voice is not heard. In all the billion-trillion stars, in every galaxy, every universe, every realm, every dimension and in any timeline, there is NO PLACE where their frequency, PROCLAIMING WHO YOU REALLY ARE, AND CALLING YOU INTO, IS NOT HEARD!!!! DO YOU UNDERSTAND THIS?!? WOOWWW, THANK YOU, JESUS!

These stars are WITNESSES of what your original blueprint is! These stars/planets are connected to your inheritance and, therefore, that are always FIGHTING FOR YOU! From their God given courses, they are fighting for you, declaring who you are, proclaiming it day after day and night after night.

Judges 5:20: This is when Deborah went to war against Sisera and looked at what it's saying in the Aramaic translation.

v5..." From the heavens, THEY fought, THE STARS (KAKKO - stars, NOT angels ... Mallek) ... FROM THEIR COURSES THEY FOUGHT against Sisera."

You guys, THE STARS HAVE A VOICE and the stars that have not traded with lucifer, the stars that have NOT left their GOD-GIVEN COURSE, they WILL ALWAYS, ALWAYS point you back to their Creator, Elohim, Adonai, our Father, and proclaim who we REALLY ARE!

Do you wonder why the ones operating in the kingdom in darkness know so much more about the stars than we do? Because we've been freaking out about it. I am NOT speaking in this book about astrology, I am speaking about astronomy, which is totally different! We do NOT worship the stars! We do not worship angels, spirit beings, men in white linen, cloud of witnesses. We do not worship anything else BUT God the Father, Yeshua and Holy Spirit. However, we do understand that we CAN engage with ALL that is part of our inheritance, as they were all created to help us walk out our blueprint! Just because I engage and communicate with you, does not mean I am worshiping you! Just because I engage with the voice of MY INHERITANCE, does not mean I am worshiping them! Just because I engage with the angels attached to my blueprint, does not mean I am worshiping them! IF that was the case, that means we have all been guilty of worshiping demons, every time we told them to get lost! We have a cloud of witnesses who are there on our behalf. We have angelic hosts who are there on our behalf, all that is in creation that has not traded with lucifer are here on our behalf to help us step into who we really are supposed to be, so we can restore order back into them ... they are part of our inheritance! So, all of these beings, no matter what they are, again, IF they have not traded with lucifer, will ALWAYS point us back to who we are IN AND THROUGH JESUS! THEY WILL NEVER EVER want worship, but ALWAYS POINT US BACK TO Adonai and our original blueprint...That IS their mandate!

Let's go back to Abraham. Like I said in the book earlier, very little is told in the Bible of Abraham's early life. Except for a few hints here and there, hardly anything is told of him in the Torah or the New Testament of him until he was seventy-five years old.

Such important events of Abraham's life ... his birth, his very close walk with YHVH, his defiance of Nimrod (the king and leader of all the heathens and idol worshippers who had Abraham thrown into a burning furnace) is only hinted in the Torah. The full story of Abraham's early life was only told by word of mouth from rabbis, from generation to generation, until the details were finally recorded by the Sages of the Talmud in various historical records. One such historical record is the Book of Jasher. In these historical records, there are some interesting details about Abraham's early life, spanning from his youth until he reached the age of seventy-five.

Abraham (who was first called Abram) was born in the year 1948 after Creation (1813 BCE). According to one tradition, he was born in the month of Nissan. According to another tradition, he was born in the month of Tishrei. His father's name was Terah, who was seventy years old when Abraham was born. Abraham's mother's name was Amathlaah. The town in which he was born was called Cutha, in Mesopotamia. In the Torah (Old Testament), Abraham's birthplace is called Ever-haNahar ("Beyond the River").

Abraham was the tenth generation removed from Noah, being a direct descendant of Shem, Noah's son. Shem was the father of all the "Semitic" peoples. When Abraham was born, Shem was 390 years old, and his father, Noah, was 892 years old. WOW! AMAZING, right?!? Abraham was 58 years old when Noah died. Now remember how I said earlier that Abraham spent quite a few years with Noah and Shem, being mentored by them, here are the details. Terah, Abraham's father, was the chief officer or minister of King Nimrod of Babylon and unfortunately, he was also an idol worshipper, like his king, and their chief god was the Sun.

Now, Nimrod's soothsayer knew the heavens and the voice of the heavens, and they understood it. Because of that understanding, they saw something very powerful happening in the heavens and they freaked out. A big star appeared in the heavens, coming from the East and it began to eat up the four stars that were connected to Nimrod's ability to read the future from demonic revelation and it just stayed there.

These soothsayers knew that something BIG was coming and it was much bigger than anything that Nimrod carried. They also understood who that star was representing. They went to Nimrod telling him that Terah's newly born son would one day be a danger to his throne. Of course, Nimrod ordered Terah to bring him the baby when he is born, to be put to death. Terah, however, was not about to do that, so he tricked the king. Instead of taking his real son to the king, he took the baby of a slave, who was born on the same night as Abraham, and Nimrod killed the baby with his own hands, believing that he was now safe from the threat.

Terah took baby Abraham, with his mother and nurse and hid them in a cave for ten years. At the age of three years, Abraham knew that it was silly to worship the sun or any other idol, because there was a great God who created the sun and the moon, and the whole world, who, though this God, was unseen. Abraham, from this young age, also knew that this real unseen God, knew everything, and He is the real King of the World, more powerful than Nimrod. Since that time, Abraham's faith in this unseen and unknown God grew stronger every day. During his time in the cave, his mom would tell Abraham about his relatives, Noah and Shem. She told Abraham how Noah and Shem knew this God in a very unique and personal way, and Abraham desired very much to know them and learn about this unseen God from them.

At the age of ten, Abraham decided to leave the cave and to go to live with these relatives that his mother told him about. Unknown to anybody, Abraham made his way from the low country to the mountainous region of Ararat, in the land of Kedem, where Noah and his family lived. He was made welcome by old Noah and Shem, who taught him all they knew about God and the ways of God. They showed Abraham the hidden mysteries of YHVH and Abraham knew God in such a close way, like nobody during that time. Abraham learned how to engage and go into God. As he did that, he went into the timeline of God, going all the way to the beginning, seeing it and going in the future ... seeing it, and doing some incredible things. All of this BECAUSE of his relationship with Adonai.

Remember in Genesis 14:17-24 when Abraham meets Melchizedek after Abraham won the war. We can see that Abraham recognized Melchizedek from somewhere! How did he KNOW who Melchizedek was before there was a nation of Israel? How did he know TO GIVE which Melchizedek a tenth?

Let's look at the scripture in the NIV...

v.17 After Abram returned from his victory over Kedorlaomer and all his allies, the king of Sodom went out to meet him in the valley of Shaveh (that is, the King's Valley).

v.18 And Melchizedek, the king of Salem and a priest of God Most High, [a] brought Abram some bread and wine. 19 Melchizedek blessed Abram with this blessing: v.20 b...Then Abram gave Melchizedek a tenth of all the goods he had recovered.

I believe that Abraham met Melchizedek when he was IN the timeline of God, in the city of Zion, the mountain of God. You see, he knew that Melchizedek was the chief chancellor of the treasury storehouse of Heaven, from his encounter with him Melchizedek in the City of Zion. That is why Abraham gave him a tenth. He traded into him because he knew once he traded with Melchizedek. He was trading for Isaac and Jacob. He was trading for and into his future generations. I go in more detail on this subject in the Unveiling the Trading Floors book.

Abraham stayed with Noah and Shem for about 39 years, until the year 1997. It was at the end of this period, when he was 48 years old, while still at Noah's house, that Abraham heard about the world-shattering event of the Tower of Babel, which took place in the land of Shinar, where Nimrod reigned supreme. Nimrod and his people wanted to build a tower that would reach up to Heaven, like I stated earlier, to try to get to God without a relationship, out of demonic revelation.

We saw that God came down and put the kibosh on that plan! When Abraham heard the craziness Nimrod was doing, he got quite ticked off and decided that it was high time for him to go out and teach them the truth about God, and about the falsehood and worthlessness of the idols. He knew that in defying Nimrod, and even his own father, he would be risking his life, for Nimrod had proclaimed himself god and demanded that all the people worship him. At the age of 50 (in the year 1998), Abraham returned to his father's house in Babylon finding that his father, Terah, was a high priest of the idol worshippers. NICE, Terah! He had twelve chief gods, one for each month of the year. In fact, there was a worship place in Terah's house, where idols of wood, stone, silver, and gold were made. People came to offer sacrifices to these idols, or to buy them, and Terah had a thriving business. Terah appointed Abraham to be the salesman and take charge of the business. You can imagine what a great help Abraham was to his dad's business... hahah, NOT!

Abraham's activities, in words and deeds, made Nimrod a tad angry. Both Abraham and his father were ordered to appear before the king. Here, the king's stargazers at once recognized Abraham was the one about whom they had warned the king. Terah was going to be put to death for deceiving the king, and he put the blame on his older son Haran, who was 32 years older than Abraham. Nimrod ordered that Abraham be thrown into a burning furnace, telling Abraham, "I will destroy you with fire". Abraham response to him was brilliant, saying, "My God is the God of fire and your fire will not touch me!"

So, he placed Abraham in the fiery furnace. Now, what is really interesting is that this furnace where Abraham was placed was the same furnace in which Shadrach, Meshach, and Abednego were placed, because this was the only furnace back then that they were able to heat it up to 10 times the normal heat. For THREE days, Nimrod would walk and look in the fire and would see Abraham just walking in that fire! He did this day one, day two, and, finally, on day three, Nimrod went to the mouth of the furnace calling Abraham to come out! When the people saw this, they began to worship Abraham, but he told them to worship God, a perfect opportunity for Abraham to introduce his God to them.

Nimrod was greatly afraid of Abraham, CLEARLY, and he RECOGNIZED that the God of Abraham is truly a great God! He gave Abraham many precious gifts, among them Eliezer, a member of the king's household, who became Abraham's trusted servant and friend. (To read more about Abraham and his times, go to The Book of Jasher or to the Chabad International writings.)

Guys, do you understand that whenever death and chaos SEES THE AUTHENTIC POWER AND TRUE NATURE OF A MATURE SON, IT WILL ACKNOWLEDGE IT AND BOW TO IT! Why? Because you carry a higher frequency than what chaos and death carry!

Listen, when you take a tuning fork and you hit it, it creates a frequency and a vibration and anything that's of a lesser vibrational frequency MUST come UNDER and SUBMIT to THAT SOUND, THE SOUND OF THE HIGHER VIBRATIONAL FREQUENCY, UNTIL IT STARTS TO TAKE ON THAT SOUND!

Watch this. Something happened between Genesis chapter 1:1 and Genesis chapter 1:2. We see in verse 1 that everything is good. We see that God created the heavens and the earth, so that was good, because everything that God creates is always good. However, in verse 2, we see that something has happened, and it caused there to be an earth without form and void. It became a waste and emptiness, filled by a thick blanket of darkness that not only covered the earth but also covered the face of the deep. So, on the first day, everything was great, and on the second day, it was chaotic and dark. I want to suggest to you that this is when lucifer was cast out of heaven for his unrighteous trading. When he was cast out of heaven, he brought chaos and the darkness he was operating in, in all of God's creation! That is why all of THAT is groaning and looking for us to awaken and take back YHVH's order!

Did you know that they have seen that Mars HAD an atmosphere, but something happened that caused Mars to be in this chaotic stage that it is in. They have observed this fact on different planets as well. AGAIN, EVERYTHING THAT GOD CREATES IS GOOD AND HAS AN ORDER THERE IS NO CHAOS WHEN GOD CREATES SOMETHING!

Now, as we continue to look in verse 2, we see that the Spirit of God was hovering over the earth, over the face of the waters, and over of the face of the deep. Another translation for HOVERING is BROODING which means to "SHAKING, MOVING, FLUTTERING ... VIBRATE". Why? Look at this. So, here's the chaos and this chaos is covering the earth. Now, chaos carries a totally different frequency than that of God, than that of the ORIGINAL BLUEPRINT that God PUT INSIDE the waters of the deep, and also placed over the earth. The Lord knew that in order for the original blueprint to come forth, the original FREQUENCY of what He meant the earth to be, that was now covered by the chaotic frequency, He would have to go OVER THE EARTH, OVER THE WATERS OF THE DEEP, AND BROOD, OR VIBRATE, over them! Why? He would have to vibrate OVER IT, until the lower frequency of chaos that was covering the earth, that was IN the waters of the deep, would COME UNDER SUBMISSION TO THE HIGHER FREQUENCY OF GOD, AND HIS ORIGINAL BLUEPRINT! At that point, that which was hidden, covered by chaos, would HEAR THAT FREQUENCY OF YHVH BREAKING LOOSE and it would break out from under the control of the chaotic frequency, and begin to SHINE! The arc was formed FROM HEAVEN TO EARTH, releasing the original blueprint that has been covered in chaos and destruction

Remember what I said at the beginning? The Kingdom of God will NOT come upon anything that does not look like it! So, there are times where the Spirit of the Lord has to come and vibrate over certain situations, which will FORCE any other lower frequency to bow its knee to the higher frequency. As it does that, it releases the SHADOW that God is looking for, that which was covered by chaos, so that He can release the ORIGINAL in and through a person, situation or place.

Now, back to Genesis 1. After the Spirit of the Lord vibrated over the waters of the deep, we see that God said, "Let there be LIGHT!" Now, God said this BEFORE He created the sun, that actually is the one that GIVES the literal light! What light was He speaking to? The ORIGINAL LIGHT that is IN the ORIGINAL BLUEPRINT, in the original record of what GOD said the earth should be! Now, also notice something else that is VERY interesting and powerful. Notice that God SPOKE to the earth to bear the seeds for trees, plants, and vegetation in chapter 1, v. 11, and ALL these come forth from the ground WITHOUT THE LIGHT AND ENERGY OF THE SUN, because the sun and the stars were not brought forth YET! SO, how in the world did all these things come forth that we know need the light and energy of the SUN in order to grow and survive?

When the earth was NO LONGER BOUND BY LIMITATION OF CHAOS, operating in a false CHAOTIC blueprint but was now operating OUT OF THE creatiVE LIGHT that is IN the original blueprint, that frequency that creates broke forth and it created!

There is no limitation or boundaries that hold us to the confines of the "laws of nature" because we are operating outside of that, from within "CHRIST IN ME"! What I am trying to show you here is that when you are operating out of your original blueprint, ALL that is attached to your original blueprint that carries the CREATIVE LIGHT OF GOD ... THAT ALWAYS CREATED ... will create all that is needed! Do you understand that all that the earth needed in order to become what IT WAS SUPPOSED to be came from the ORIGINAL BLUEPRINT?!

We see that in verse 14 and 15 that He made the sun and the stars "...and let them be useful as lights in the expanse of the heavens TO PROVIDE LIGHT ON THE EARTH...16...God made the two great lights - the greater light ... the sun to rule the day, and the lesser light ... to rule the night." The earth brought forth the trees and all vegetation OUT OF THE LIGHT THAT WAS COMING FORTH FROM THE ORIGINAL BLUEPRINT, NOT from the energy of the sun, because He created the sun and stars in verse 14 and 15. WHEN YOU WALK OUT YOUR ORIGINAL BLUEPRINT, NOTHING STANDS IN YOUR WAY FOR MANIFESTING ALL THAT IS IN YOUR ORIGINAL BLUEPRINT!

Now, let me continue to unpack this amazing mystery that He is revealing. So, you and I are 78% water! So, there are waters of the deep IN YOU as well! Watch this. Like I said, the Kingdom of God is inside of you. When you understand that the Kingdom of God that is inside of your spirit man is a portal, a gate, or entry point for you to access and enter the Kingdom of Heaven, Mount Zion, the city of our God and, by FAITH, you CHOOSE to do just that, something takes place. Remember, the Kingdom of God "is at hand". It is as close to you as the air that you breathe ... all you need to do it CHOOSE to engage YOUR DESIRE of going and seeing Jesus and ALLOW the eyes of your spirit (aka your GOD GIVEN IMAGINATION) to paint YOUR DESIRE and engage that! As you do that, you are engaging the presence of H'ashem, through the eyes of your spirit, your imagination, BY FAITH.

Now, when you are in that place, INSIDE THAT frequency and, as you CHOOSE to allow and engage THAT frequency, it will begin to HOVER, BROOD ... to VIBRATE OVER YOU and the waters of YOUR deep, it will vibrate until the frequency of the false blueprint that you have been operating in and out of bows its knee to YHVH's frequency and the LIGHT of your original blueprint will begin to FLOW OUT OF YOU. As it does, it will begin to unfold and create the desire of the Father for WHO YOU ARE, and the unlocking of your Destiny Scrolls will begin to unfold little by little, allowing you to walk them out! AGAIN, what we have seen happening in Genesis, will happen in, for, and through you! That creaTIVE light of YHVH that is inside your original blueprint ... that light will begin to flow out of you and, THAT light, will create everything that is WRITTEN in that record! You will no longer rely on and be bound by the laws of this world or this realm! You will no longer be bound by the limitation of this false reality, and the mutations in your DNA that have brought about a counterfeit of who you really are, what your bloodline is supposed to be, supposed to carry, and supposed to release! You will no longer continue to create your "reality" from the source of the experiences ... from the memories of every trade, every sin, every event that was NOT written in the Original Blueprint and, thereby, passing that down to your children's children! You will operate OUTSIDE of that because THAT IS NO LONGER THE SOURCE OF YOUR SUPPLY, OR THE SOURCE OF YOUR SURVIVAL! You will operate from the GREATEST FORMS OF ENERGY AND POWER AND THAT WILL BECOME THE SOURCE OR YOUR SUPPLY; TO CREATE WHAT WAS ALWAYS IN HIS HEART FOR YOU AND YOUR BLOODLINE!!

Back to Abraham ... As I mentioned a bit earlier, Abraham developed such a close relationship with The Father and, through it, he understood the original blueprint of things that God made and shaped. He had an understanding of the blueprint, of the pattern of God, that has been lost. Because he KNEW ADONAI, ADONAI started showing Abraham things that not many had seen. He SAW his original blueprint and he understood that when he would step in THAT, he would step into the timeline of God! Do you understand? When you are in God, literally BY FAITH, you DESIRE to be in Him and you CHOOSE, BY FAITH, TO SEE, or sense yourself IN HIM. You are, then, outside of time and space and every, every situation that has bound you to chaos.

Before I continue with Abraham, let me share an encounter I had a few years ago. In the encounter, Jesus was teaching me how to step inside of Him, what it means to step in Him, and what I can do in and through Him. The encounter started with me entering the garden of my heart to meet with Jesus. That's where I love to meet him because I just LOVE flowers and I love being in a garden. So, I have created this garden in my heart specifically with flowers and things that I know

Jesus loves. Again, EVERYTHING MUST be based on LOVE to build a deeper relationship with Jesus, with the Father, and Holy Spirit. REMEMBER, and please keep in mind, that everything you hear, see, and sense must, must, must start out of a desire for relationship, relationship, relationship, relationship, relationship!

So, from the garden, as Jesus was sharing some things with me, He began to show me how to step into Him. He said to me," Corina, it is a choice that comes out of a deep desire, and it is all done by faith. Do you desire to step into me?" I answered Him with eyes full of tears and said, "Oh, Jesus, YES … I want to ALWAYS be in you. I never want to be apart from you! How do I do it?" All of a sudden, He opened Himself up like you would open up a long coat that is on you, and He said, "Now, Corina, let your desire to step into me, draw you in me."

I saw myself stepping inside of Him, and I turned so that I was looking out through His eyes. We began to fly and, all of a sudden, we were out in the cosmos. The planets seemed very tiny as we were out there, but the closer we flew towards them, the bigger those planets got until we flew past them, and they became tiny again. It did not seem like we flew for a long time. However, all of a sudden, we found ourselves in a place where it was completely dark … and not one star or planet was seen. I looked, and there was the Father. He was extremely huge. He was big enough for me to see the length of him. As we approached Him, the Father said, "Corina, do you understand that when you are in Yeshua, because He and I are one, when you are in Him, you also have access to be in me! When you are in Him, you can do all things through Him, but that is not all that you can do! When you are in ME, you can then do EVERYTHING that I can!"

All of a sudden, He opened Himself up like a gate inviting me to go in Him. As I went into Him, I was now looking out through the eyes of the Father! As I was looking out through His eyes, I saw nothing but this vast darkness; no planets, no stars, nothing. I said, "Daddy, where is everything?" He opened His hand and told me to look. Again, remember, I was looking out through His eyes. As I looked in His hand, I saw what looked like a clear glass capsule. He said to me, "Corina, everything that I have made ... earth, everything on it, under it, and over it ... every planet, every star, every galaxy, every universe, every dimension (even time and space) is here, in the palm of my hand, in this capsule. Inside this capsule is also every power, rulership, authority that my enemies and your enemies have. Death is also limited and bound in this capsule as is every law that has bound you to every limitation. Now, Corina, when you take your rightful position IN Yeshua and IN ME, tell me, where are you located?"

Words cannot describe what was going on in me as the Father was showing me this powerful truth! I was trying to grasp the reality of what He was trying to show me and, before I was really able to think clearly, He continued with an answer to the question He posed for me before "Corina, when you are in me, you are OUTSIDE of all of that! You are outside of time and space. That means you are outside of the timeline that is limiting you to IT! That means that you can go back in time and correct a wrong, that will then change the present and the future! I WANT YOU TO BE A HISTORY MAKER AND A HISTORY CHANGER! I am looking for the ones that CHOOSE to do just that! When you are in me, you can grab who I said you are to be, from the future and pull THAT into your present! Like Paul, like King David, you can NOW live your present out of your future! If you understand this ability and you choose to step into it, the laws that have bound you to the dictates of the chaotic situation that is in your present will no longer be the source of your supply! Since you have learned and chosen to step in ME, outside of 'time', pulling your future into your present, that will make your present look like your future which mirrors your beginning, your Original blueprint!"

"Now, when you are in me, you are OUTSIDE of the reach of all powers, principalities, rulers operating in darkness. You are outside of any disease, chaos, and death. Do you understand? When you are in me, you are FAR ABOVE all of that and those powers that are limited and enclosed in the capsule that is in my hand. Therefore, it is in your hand! Are you beginning to understand how important it is for you NOT ONLY TO KNOW your position but for you to CHOOSE TO STEP INTO IT BY FAITH THROUGH YOUR DESIRE TO BE IN

Yeshuah ... TO BE IN ME?!" I was in awe, tears streaming down my face, wanting so much to just hug Him and not wanting to let go. I just have to say that my love for Jesus is literally like the love a child has for her big brother that she so looks up to, that she adores, and for the Father is this deep childlike love that a little girl would have for her daddy. My faith is the same as ... well, if He tells me to do ANYTHING, as long as I know that it is He who is asking me, I will do it! I have that childlike faith and childlike love; NOT CHILDISH, CHILD LIKE. There is a huge difference. Allow yourself to step into that childlike love and childlike faith and, as you do, I can tell you that there is no limit what He will do with and through you!

Clearly, He knew and felt my childlike, insane desire to love on Him as my daddy, so He proceeded to tell me something that blew me away! "Corina, you can hug me and squeeze on me any time you want! Remember that, if you are in me, I am, therefore, in YOU! So, when you hug your arm, you are hugging me! Your body IS MY TEMPLE! Love it, take care of it and, as you do that, you are loving and taking care of me!"

Wow, I would have a lot to say right here, however, I will hold it for another time, but I do what to say this one thing. When I was so blessed to host Ian Clayton here in Nashville, on our third time hosting him, he spoke on how important it is for us to love our bodies ... not in a twisted way but stepping out of the lie that our body is bad ... a dirty vessel ... because all that God cares about is our soul and spirit. I was blown away as Ian was talking about it because I knew that that is what YHVH was trying to teach me four years prior in the encounter I have shared with you above. Love your body, and as you love it by taking care of it, you ARE loving on the Father and taking care of His temple!

There was more He was teaching me in this encounter; however, I will leave the more for another time. I wanted you to understand that there IS an amazing position that we have access to. However, it is our choice to step into it or not. I also wanted you to understand how BIG YOU REALLY ARE when you are IN YOUR POSITION! You are outside of the reach of the enemy, and all that have chosen to operate with him, against God and His children! I want to encourage you to take a few moments to SEE and to MEDITATE on this powerful truth! To "meditate" means to chew like a cow, or like a sheep chews grass. It also means to IMAGINE and to SEE it! Do you see yourself INSIDE the capsule or do you see yourself IN YHVH? Remember the scripture I keep mentioning? IF (a choice) any man be IN CHRIST, he is [THEN] A NEW CREATION! That's where Abraham, Moses, and David were! David did not just go out into the field playing his harp. David realized the access He had to God THROUGH HIS worship, into the heart of God, that was birthed out of his LOVE for God! David was a man after God's heart. He so pursued God's heart until he found it, and he learned to LIVE FROM THAT PLACE, and to reflect that, into his existence! From that place, the heart of God, David then had access to the timeline of God, not only seeing his future from there, but he pulled his future, like Paul, into his present. Listen, that is how David KNEW that he would be king! So, when the lion, the bear, and even Saul came after him, because David saw his future, he KNEW that "You bear, you lion, Saul, you are not going to be able to kill me BECAUSE I SAW THAT I WILL BE KING!" As Ian Clayton would often say, "IF you know your future, your present cannot kill you!" I want to add to that and say to you that if you know your future, the dictates of the laws, and that the chaotic atmosphere around you IS NO LONGER GOING TO BE THE SOURCE OF YOUR SUPPLY, and that you will no longer draw your energy from that, you will draw from the supply of energy from who God said that you are ... that is in your age to come (aka, your future). As you do that, you will be like David, like Paul, like Enoch, and like Abraham pulling that future, who you are to be, into your present; therefore, your present taking on the image of THAT...your future!

What does your future say? Meaning: What does your ORIGINAL blueprint say? Does it say that you were meant to die by disease or accident or old age? Let's look a bit at that. John 10:9 AMP. "I am the Door; anyone who enters through Me will be saved [and will live forever], and will GO IN AND OUT [freely], and find good pastures."

So, notice that, here, Jesus says that HE IS THE GATE; to enter where? Where is Jesus sitting now? At the right hand of The Father.

So where is that? IN the Kingdom of Heaven, in the ABODE of GOD, IN Mount Zion, the City of our God! So, who is the gate for us to enter IN that place?

"Oh, I will see heaven, I will see the angels, I will see beyond the veil, I will see Jesus, I will see the Father, but I have to wait until I am dead because, you know, no one sees The Father without dying!" I think we ALL have said this! If you found yourself saying this and believing this, then WHO JUST becomes the gate for you? DEATH. In John 10:9, WHO did Jesus say that is the gate INTO heaven? HE IS..NOT DEATH!

So, guess what He is saying ... "Death is NOT your entry gate into ALL that the Father has for you!" Let's break it down even more. If you would have to DIE before you can ENTER into LIVING FOREVER, how can a dead person GO IN AND OUT, and find good pastures?

Hmmm....do you see how we have made a covenant and traded on the demonic floor with the spirit of death? Then, we wonder why everything around us seems to be dying...relationships, finances, joy, health, and so on.

Now, let's look a bit deeper. Jesus says here that HE IS the gate and WHOSOEVER CHOOSES to enter THROUGH HIM not only shall LIVE FOREVER (like meaning...now shall be able to live forever, NOT when you die...not your body dies but your spirit shall live forever) but shall also go IN AND OUT and FIND GOOD PASTURES! What good pastures is He talking about?

Let's go to Psalm 23 ... The Lord is my shepherd. I shall not want. He makes me lie down in green pastures. (Again, what pasture? The pastures IN His kingdom. The pastures IN His HEART, the most intimate place of God, where you CAN GO IN AND OUT, FREELY, finding the good pastures and, in THAT PLACE, you will LIVE FOREVER! That IS part of the entry point Jesus gave you and me, THROUGH THE CROSS!) What does it say after? "Though I walk THROUGH the valley of the SHADOW of death, I will FEAR NO

EVIL BECAUSE YOU are with (IN me and I am IN YOU)!" Now, remember I talked earlier about us needing to become a SHADOW, REFLECTING HIM in and through our "SHADOW", because God is always looking for a shadow of Himself to come upon and fill it and flow out of it.

So, again, how is a shadow made? In order for a shadow to me made, you must STAND in the presence of a greater light! As you do, you absorb that light in you and THAT LIGHT FLOWS OUT OF YOU, CREATING THE SHADOW! Do you understand?

Let's go deeper.

Psalm 91 ... "He that DWELLS IN THE SECRET PLACE of the most high ..." (What IS that SECRET PLACE? That secret place is the most INTIMATE PLACE OF GOD ... WHERE? HIS HEART ... RELATIONSHIP, RELATIONSHIP, RELATIONSHIP ... L O V E! Watch ...What happens in that secret place of God?) ... "SHALL abide under the SHADOW of His wings". So, let's break this down even more...

When you CHOOSE to go THROUGH the cross, the finished work of the cross, into the Heart of God (because you desire to build a deeper relationship with HIM), you are NOW in the PASTURES inside His heart! As you REST in these pastures, you are taking in more of who He is and that power is able to TRANSFORM YOU INTO a NEW creation...which includes you LIVING FOREVER.

From there, you have FREE access to go IN AND OUT as often as you like to those pastures, INSIDE the secret place of the most high God, which is His heart. Because you are NOW in that place, in His heart, at the very CORE, the CENTER of who He is, you are also now standing IN the most POWERFUL SOURCE OF ENERGY AND CREATIVE LIGHT, THAT CREATES ALL that is in the Father's heart! What is that? You are now standing IN the essence of who He is, which is LOVE, which IS the River of Glory. Now, because you are IN that light, you are now absorbing THAT greater light IN YOU as you are RESTING UNDER THAT SHADOW, and as you rest there, you are absorbing that light and NOW, you BECOME A SHADOW OF THAT LIGHT on earth, in your existence!!!!

Remember that, at that point, you are a carrier of THAT light, THAT shadow and that frequency, as you are FREELY able to go IN AND OUT. As you find yourself in those pastures, notice that death ONLY HAS A SHADOW ... because death was STRIPPED AT THE CROSS of all its power. Its key taken away. It was made a full spectacle of, and mockery of, and EVEN ITS STING was taken away! SO, the only thing that is left is a SHADOW!

Now, two things that I want to point out here. First, do you understand that YOU CAN ACTUALLY WALK THROUGH A SHADOW? So, notice in Psalm 23 that we are to WALK THROUGH THE SHADOW of death! We are not to freak out when we see it and allow that shadow to become the source of our supply, because, again, WHATEVER YOU FOCUS ON, MULTIPLIES IN YOUR LIFE! We are to WALK THROUGH THAT SHADOW!

LISTEN, the only way that the shadow of death can have any effect on you is IF IT SEES A SHADOW OF ITSELF. Meaning, if it sees an agreement IN you that you made with it...that is its only power! Remember, again, the only power the enemy has over us is what we give him. How do we do that? BY THE SHADOW WE CARRY AND REFLECT! The shadow you and I carry is manifested and reflected out of whatever we put our focus, our agreements, our engagements, and our faith in. Where you are seated will determine what shadow you will reflect. Are you seated IN chaos...or are you seated IN heavenly places FAR ABOVE all the chaos? Your position will give you your perspective, and the shadow that you will reflect. WHICH ONE DO YOU CHOOSE TO REFLECT?

So, if I am SEATED IN GOD THE FATHER, in the most SECRET OR SACRED, intimate place of God, His heart, and I absorb IN my BEING THAT greater light, my focus being on HIM and on THAT light, I then come into agreement with THAT! Now, because I have chosen to step there and I come into agreement with who He is and who He said that I am IN and THROUGH HIM, I AM

NOW a shadow of THAT VICTORY OVER DEATH!! So, THOUGH I WALK THROUGH THE SHADOW OF the valley of DEATH, I FEAR NO EVIL BECAUSE I NOW CARRY THE VERY FREQUENCY, THE VERY SOUND, THE VERY POWER OF YHVH THAT DEFEATED DEATH at and THROUGH the cross! I now walk THROUGH IT, onto the other side where He, my Daddy, has prepared a banquet table for me! He prepared this banquet table for me before my enemies and He is making them watch, as He elevates me, and places me in my rightful place. This place is far above all the powers, rulers, kings, dominions, evil spirits ... all that have stood against me and my bloodline! Do you understand who you really are?

Let's go back to Genesis 15:5 and read again what this scripture says. AMP. v5. And He brought him outside or brought him FORTH ABROAD [his tent INTO the starlight] (INTO the light given by stars) and said, "Look now TOWARDS the heavens and TELL them if you are able to number them."

Now, NOTICE, God brought ABRAHAM OUTSIDE, or God brought Abraham ABROAD, INTO the light given by stars! From that place, the Lord told him, "Look now TOWARDS." "Towards" does not mean stretching your neck up and looking up. It means, facing the area ahead and near. Now, the word "ABROAD" means, "going INTO a foreign land or another continent or reality. Out of ONE door or one place into another."

So, we have been reading this scripture with our linear, Greek understanding and we think that God called Abraham out of his tent that he was living in, out in the desert and he told him, "C'mon Abraham, stretch your neck and look up ... now, try to count those stars!" That is NOT what the rabbis taught.

Now, the following is what the rabbis' oral traditions said, and this is what was passed down from generation to generation and later written down in Aramaic. The rabbis said that God brought Abraham ABROAD, OUT OF ONE REALITY ... his TERRESTRIAL tent (meaning his body). Remember that the Word says that your body is the TENT, TABERNACLE or temple of the Holy Spirit. So, they taught that God brought Abraham out of the reality of the terrestrial, his tent or body, out of one door of a reality INTO another door, or another realm, land, continent or reality ... Into what? God brought him forth ABROAD, INTO the STARLIGHT, into the light given by stars, so, into the CELESTIAL. From THAT position, God told Abraham to look TOWARDS, meaning AHEAD OF HIM, facing the area ahead and NEAR him. Again, this was NOT meaning to look up, but look directly ahead of him in the area close to him and to TELL THE STARS (so, talk to the stars) and tell THEM if he can actually count them! WOW, this is a TOTALLY different dimension of this scripture is it not?

God positioned Abraham in the heavens, in the LIGHT OF THE STARS, and through his story, God has been trying to teach us something very important. Unfortunately, in the body of Christ we have NOT understood the precedent set by God through Abraham.

Listen, IF UNDER THE OLD COVENANT God was able to place a man IN the celestial in order to FACILITATE AND bring to earth the BLUEPRINT of the Kingdom of Heaven and God's Desire for humanity, for earth, and all of creation, HOW MUCH MORE CAN AND SHOULD WE, UNDER THE NEW COVENANT, which has given us the ability to be seated THERE in heavenly places with and in Jesus, do?!

Let me say it again the following way. This was before Jesus came to make a way for us to get back to our position which Adam lost by trading. So, as we see, God took a man (before Christ) and was able to place him OUTSIDE his TERRESTRIAL REALITY, out of that door, out of his "tent", INTO the reality of God, THROUGH THAT DOOR, INTO THE CELESTIAL!

How much more should you and I, because of the cross, be able to do just that, and more? How much more should we be able to get OUT of this carnal, chaotic reality that is around us and be able to step outside of it and INTO our position, getting HIS perspective that is FAR ABOVE what the chaos in the terrestrial atmosphere says?

REMEMBER, WHATEVER YOU LOOK TO MULTIPLIES AND BECOMES THE SOURCE OF YOUR SUPPLY!

What CAN God do with a man or a woman that chooses to engage IN THE heart of the Father? Oh, my goodness!! We will become unstoppable and the enemy knows that! That is why he wants to keep us bound to limitations that the spirit of religion puts on us; that spirit of religion that is working hand in hand with the antichrist spirit.

SHIFT THE ILLUSION INTO HIS REALITY

I said this a bit earlier, but I will repeat it. The problem is that religious spirits working hand in hand with the antichrist spirit, have so controlled the governmental arenas of the churches. They've told you what to think, believe, become, do, and not do. IF you dare talk about things that reflect the reality of all you have been given access to, like going to heaven NOW, not waiting until you die ... IF you dare to talk about the angels who have been assigned to help you walk out your blueprint, and their names, other beings assigned to you by God ... if you speak of the supernatural power that you KNOW you have THROUGH the cross that has been given to you THROUGH the Covenant of Adoption, which includes never having to die a physical death, you are called a heretic, operating in demonic powers, a witch, and worse, bullied to stop you at all cost!

It is sad that every time we talk about the supernatural promises of Christ and His abilities that we have, and we are supposed to be walking in and doing now, not when we die, the religious demons give credit to the devil! SOMETHING IS WRONG IF we think and if we credit all these supernatural abilities and powers to the enemy and his allies!!!

We're preaching the gospel BUT denying THE POWER! Let me tell you something. The spirit man knows that there's something more ... that you were created FOR MORE! (How many of you are sitting there getting stirred up with excitement "I know there is more!") Depression, hopelessness, suicidal thoughts, and suicidal acts happen because the spirit KNOWS there is SO MUCH MORE available than what the soul and body is experiencing, and the spirit man is CRYING OUT FOR THE MORE! "I WAS CREATED FOR MORE! I can't find it... I CAN'T FIND IT... where is it?! This is not all that I am to be. THIS IS NOT ALL I AM TO DO!" Do you understand? The spirit man is in SPIRITUAL AMNESIA, FEELING that there is something MORE to who he/she is! Now, because some of the churches are preaching JUST the gospel, BUT DENYING THE POWER, teaching only religion and everything connected to those regulations, there is the problem! Deny the POWER IN the word that literally transforms us from the inside out, now, not when we die, and you have a FALSE GOSPEL! THAT IS the doctrine of demons! There is no way the enemy wants you to KNOW who you really are! So, he absolutely does not have any issue using the Bible to PUT YOU IN A BOX and, also, put the resurrection power of Jesus Christ in that box as well! The enemy knows the Bible forwards and backwards! He will use it to control and confine you IF the power IN the word is manipulated or left out! And, thankfully, it often is.

Also, just teaching the historical views of the Bible through preaching is NOT preaching the entire gospel! Though it is good to teach the historical reality found in the Bible, BUT, IF we PARK THERE, that is where the problem lies. As I have said from the beginning, the Word is more than all these things! The Word is full of living beings sent forth to ACCOMPLISH WHAT THEY WERE SENT TO DO being FULL OF POWER! It is of utmost importance that we recognize that and engage with them, uniting in ALL the abilities we have been given to see His will manifest in us, and in all of creation!

Some churches are GREAT at introducing the people to Jesus as their Savior, and God as our Father, and that is WONDERFUL. However, they stop there! They control the people through lies and fear, saying that the people are not to seek after tangible experiences because those will only happen after death and if one does go after them, they are deceived and in danger of losing their salvation. Lies, lies, LIES! I hope that by the time you are on this page, you see things differently and will never allow yourself to be manipulated and controlled by these principalities standing in the gateway that JESUS GAVE YOU THE RIGHT TO ENTER, NOW!

What then happens to the people that do allow themselves to be controlled and lied to? These people are going on a search to find "the MORE" that their spirit is crying out for and because the church said there is nothing more on this side of the veil, the enemy is ALWAYS

RIGHT THERE with a counterfeit, ready to engage, BECAUSE THE CHURCH DID NOT PRESENT THE ORIGINAL ... THE MORE! That is why so many of the youth and young adults (but not limited to them) are in dark occultic practices because the Church is DENYING THE SUPERNATURAL POWER OF GOD, OPERATING IN AND THROUGH US, NOW ... NOT WHEN WE DIE! We are supernatural beings craving supernatural experiences!

So, we have people who have traded with all kinds of principalities because they needed to fill the VOID that was there because of the lack of knowledge of their original blueprint (AKA ...WHO THEY REALLY ARE) leading them to more void, hopelessness, all kind of addictions, identity crises, and demonic bondages and, for some, suicide seems to be their "awakening" out of the misery they feel they are in. For people that are continuing to stay in the church, in misery, hopelessness, despair, addictions, and, again, for some, suicide seems to be the only way. WHY? They have stayed in churches that have spoken OVER and INTO them that death is the way to their total victory. They are taught for them to be ALL God said that they can be and do all that the Bible said that they can do, total victory, happiness, no more carrying the cross, no more tears, no more pain, seeing Jesus and The Father face-to-face, and the ability to be a supernatural being like Jesus is, they must die! I know this is heavy, but, unfortunately, this is the truth, and WE MUST ALLOW TRUTH TO CHANGE US!

Listen, we ARE IN A NEW AGE! Even THAT does NOT belong to the enemy. It belongs to YHVH, so, therefore, it belongs to US! What is this new age? AS HE IS NOW, SO AM I, IN THIS WORLD!

Now, let's look at the people who would NEVER want to hear about Christianity or step foot in a church. I am talking about people who are trapped in the new age arena and all kinds of branches of witchcraft, because, again, unfortunately, the church is presenting something dead. Like I stated above, we are told that death is the entry point into the Kingdom of our God, into the Kingdom of OUR FATHER! Are you kidding me?! They don't want that. They want life. We ARE already DEAD, for we HAVE (past tense), NOT WILL BE (future tense) but we HAVE BEEN CRUCIFIED WITH CHRIST AND NOW, WE ARE ... NOT WILL BE ... RESURRECTED IN CHRIST! Galatians 2:20 Amplified Bible (AMP) v.20 "I have been crucified with Christ [that is, in Him, I have shared His crucifixion]; it is no longer I who live, but Christ lives in me. The life I NOW live in the body I live BY FAITH [by adhering to, relying on, and completely trusting] IN (IN) THE Son of God, who loved me and gave Himself up for me." Pretty clear, is it not?

Justin Abraham said something that was quite powerful and, man, did it paint a clear picture of the issue I have been discussing here! He said, "Have you noticed how most churches, especially the old ones, have graveyards right on their ground or right next to them?" WOW...interesting, don't you think?

I know I am about to repeat this for, probably, the fourth time but, again, my purpose for writing these books and for teaching these amazing things that I myself am learning is to REALLY SHOW YOU WHO YOU ARE, and that this is NOT about only one or a few special people that can do this, but this is for YOU AS WELL! This is for WHOSOEVER CHOOSES to see, believe, and step into their true identity (aka, their original blueprint)!

So, again, death is NOT our entry point into the Kingdom of God. Death is NOT our entry point to see and engage His angels that were created to come alongside us and help bring forth the Father's desire in and through you and your bloodline! Death is NOT our entry TO RESURRECTION, ETERNAL, AND EVERLASTING LIFE! Death is NOT our entry point into full and total victory! Death is NOT our entry point into TRANSFORMATION AND TRANSFIGURATION! If we ever believed this, we have unwillingly and unknowingly made a covenant with death, as we began to trade on death's trading floor that works hand in hand with Apollyon and his trading floor (who is the destroyer) as well as other demonic trading floors. Like I said, then we wonder why there is so much death and destruction and hopelessness all around us. JESUS, HIS BLOOD, AND BODY, THE CROSS IS THE ENTRY POINT INTO ALL OF THESE THINGS!

Let's deal with another problem so we can get that out of the way, before we continue with Abraham. The Church, well ... let's say some of the church (because of lack of knowledge) has been teaching the people how to get the blueprint of the enemy; what he has done, what he is trying to do, or will do and then, we FRAME THAT OUT OF OUR MOUTH as we not only study it but speaking it out of our mouth! We have been taught to focus SO MUCH on the demonic! When something goes wrong, we immediately bind the so and so demon and this and the other demon, naming them and our entire conversation or "prayer" is us FOCUSING on those demons by name and binding their ability to continue to do this and the other. REMEMBER, WHATEVER YOU FOCUS ON MULTIPLIES AND BECOMES THE SOURCE OF YOUR SUPPLY!

However, lord forbid you talk to angels and, even worse, that you know their names...wow...you are a heretic because this means you are worshiping them! Hmmm...REALLY? Soooo, does that also mean that when we bind all those demons, speaking to them to get lost, we are worshiping them?

I want to show you something else. Not only does whatever you focus or look upon, look to, and give attention to multiply in you and your life ... not only does that become the source of your supply but, also, when you are focusing and looking TO something, you then are actually in its presence! Therefore, whatever you are in the presence of, YOU BECOME LIKE! Read this again, because this is HUGE!

We see it with Moses when he went up on the mountain, to be with YHVH, for 40 days.

Exodus 24:9, 10, 11-15, 30 AMP "Then Moses, Aaron, Nadab, and Abihu, and seventy of the elders of Israel went up [the mountainside] (Moses and 70 elders went up ON the literal mountain, Mount Sinai. We have seen earlier that there are overlapping dimensions with God, one portal giving entry into another dimension or portal. However, only Moses and Joshua were called to go up INTO THE MOUNTAIN OF GOD ... a totally different dimension. This is

Mount Zion, that is in the Kingdom of Heaven, the abode of YHVH) 10 and they saw [a manifestation of] the God of Israel; and under His feet there appeared to be a pavement of sapphire, just as clear as the sky itself. 11b ...and they saw [the manifestation of the presence of] God and ate and drank. 15 Then Moses went up to the mountain, and the cloud covered the mountain (the cloud IS the literal presence of YHVH which gave Moses and Joshua access into the Mountain of God, into His dimension) 16 The glory and brilliance of the LORD rested on Mount Sinai, and the cloud (of the Glory of YHVH) covered it for six days. On the seventh day God called to Moses from THE MIST OF THE CLOUD. (Where did YHVH call Moses since he was already ON mount Sinai? God called him to go UP ON the Mountain of God.) 17 In the sight of the Israelites the appearance of the glory and brilliance of the LORD was like consuming fire on the top of the mountain. 18 Moses entered the midst of the cloud AND WENT UP ON THE MOUNTAIN; and he was on the mountain forty days and forty nights. When Aharon and the people of Isra'el saw Moshe, the skin of his face was shining; and they were afraid to approach him. (The verb ירא (yara' I) is customarily translated with either to fear, to be afraid and to be in awe. This word's, verb's derivatives also is the feminine noun יראה (yir'a), meaning a fear or terror (https://www.abarim-publications.com/Dictionary).

Let's break this scripture down a bit more. Moses and the 70 elders were asked by YHVH to go up on Mount Sinai where the Cloud of His glory, His very presence, covered the top of the mountain. Now notice that Moses was called by H'ashem, from within His cloud of Glory to go UP into the Mountain of God...in the abode, the house of God.

According to the Word, what is surrounding God around His throne? The four Living Creatures! Lion, Eagle, Ox, Man. Remember, whatever you are in the presence of, you become like. Whatever you look to or look upon, whatever you focus on, becomes the source of your supply and multiplies in you!

So, because Moses was in the presence of YHVH, for 40 days and YHVH is surrounded by the powerful, glorious, creative light that emanates out of Him, He is surrounded by that FIRE that transforms. He is surrounded by the LIVING COLOR as well as by the four Living Creatures. THAT very existence of YHVH that Moses was surrounded by TRANSFORMED HIM FROM THE INSIDE, and LITERALLY TRANSFIGURED HIM ON THE OUTSIDE!

That is why the scripture says, as we looked above, in Exodus 34:30, that when he comes off the mountain, his face shined, but not shining like we think. His body became a conduit for the creatIVE light of YHVH that literally changed Moses' appearance, from the inside out. The all-powerful, CREATIVE light source of the energy of YHVH so penetrated every fiber of Moses 'body until he took on the image of what was around God and His throne...Lion, Eagle, Ox, Man! So, not only did his body absorb THAT light, making Moses a literal SHADOW and reflection of YHVH that made his face SHINE with the light of the all-consuming God, BUT his face transfigured into the four Living Creatures that are always surrounding the throne of God! As the presence and creative light force of God penetrated Moses, it changed him on the inside, transfiguring him on the outside! That is why the scripture says that the people were in TERROR ... not just in fear! They were in terror because Moses looked FREAKY, NOT human like, emanating this insanely intensive light that can consume!

Again, WHATEVER YOU ARE IN THE PRESENCE OF, YOU BECOME LIKE! That is why He is teaching us TO STEP UP IN OUR POSITION. This is what happens when we do that! Can you imagine you walking in the darkest place on the earth, under the earth, in the cosmos, in any and every dimension or timeframe, where the enemy has been ruling and, as you walk, all of a sudden, this consuming fire, this ultimate creative light source or energy and power emanates out of every cell of your body and when the enemy and his allies look at you, they see your face morphing into LION, EAGLE, OX, MAN!! TELL ME, WHO WILL MESS WITH YOU AT THAT POINT?!

Back to what church taught the intercessors. We have well-meaning intercessors sitting inside chaos, wanting to bring change in a region. So, what has been done by the group of these amazing men and women that are very well-meaning intercessors, doing only what they have learned and have been taught to do? They go study what principalities have been over that region, find out its name, and what it did and what other spirits are working with it, and what it caused. So, they start focusing on THAT. They are now studying the twisted, counterfeit blueprint and getting their directives from THAT. "Ohhh,...well this principality did this and the other, so we need to bind that and go after this other spirit that is working with this demon in the other region that is connected to this…" Because we have power in our mouth, because our BREATH creates (good, life or death) we have JUST CREATED A FRAMEWORK, THROUGH OUR MOUTH, OF A HOUSE for these things to rein-filtrate and we JUST gave them power because WE SPOKE OUT WHAT THEY DO AND THE POWERS THEY HAVE OVER THE REGION AND WHO IS WORKING WITH THEM, TO DO WHAT, IN THE REGION! Do you understand? ALSO REMEMBER, that by you focusing on it, you have just given that thing power to MULTIPLY AND NOW THAT HAS BECOME THE SOURCE OF SUPPLY FOR THAT REGION, AND NOT WHAT GOD SAID! We then wonder why the situation we have been interceding for is worse now than it was before...so we start using religious language on it by saying, "Ohhh, the enemy is just mad, and he is now retaliating."

This is a picture of what happens with anyone that is sitting in the midst of chaos, speaking to chaos eyeball to eyeball, trying to bring God in it. We canNOT bring God or His Original blueprint sitting IN chaos, sitting down here, always looking at what the enemy is doing! REMEMBER, it starts from OUR POSITION AND PERSPECTIVE FROM HEAVEN ON EARTH, NOT EARTH TO HEAVEN! Get in your position like Abraham and go get God's perspective, His blueprint, and release THAT over you, first, over your family, over your bloodline, over your neighborhood, over your city, the nation, the earth, and all of God's creation. That is how we do it, that is how we are supposed to fight!

Let me share with you a great assignment the Lord gave us, this past September, in Salem Massachusetts. This will give you a clear understanding of the difference between engaging from the heart of

Adonai, rather than engaging from chaos, in any one place, city, or any assignment that the Lord gives you.

I was spending time in the Father's heart, getting His directives for the upcoming trip that Wendy and I had to New England. I knew that there was a specific reason He wanted me to go, so I was in His heart, looking to see what He was going to show me. I knew that He would show and speak to me very clearly of what He wanted us to do on this trip, so I trusted and waited. I was working on this book, so my heart and spirit were very connected to Melchezidacha, in the midst of this coming up trip.

I arrived at Wendy's house and we were getting ready to work, when all of a sudden, she asks me, "Corina, isn't Melchezadacha connected to Salem?" Of course, she knew he was, but her question to me, completely opened up my spirit eye to SEE the plan of the Father. Oh, my goodness! All of a sudden, I had a huge download in a vision that come in a split second, hitting me so strong, that I could not talk! Electrical waves were going up and down my body, over and over and I began to cry at the reality of His presence overtaking every fiber of my being.

We were to go with a totally different mandate than many others who went to Salem. The Father was showing us all the atrocities that were done in that place, in His name, for His sake, and none of those horrors that took place in His name, had ANYTHING to do with Him or His heart.

Everything that took place in the city, referring here to the witch trials that took place in 1692, were literally brought from the kingdom in darkness, by the enemy and his demons, evil powers that were literally being "summoned" in that place because, as I will show you, the FOCUS of a certain leader, operating in Religion, Fear, Manipulation and Control, and by the horrific demonic trading floors, was bringing forth a counterfeit of the TRUE BLUE PRINT that El Elyon originally had for that city and that region!

You see, again, whatever you look to and engage with your sight, your energy and your intent in, THAT MULTIPLIES not only IN YOU, around you, around the atmosphere or the space you are in, but also, that reality you are looking to, and engaging with, THAT will become the source of your supply!

I will not get into the details of the history of these horrific so-called trials, but just briefly highlight the horrible actions that took place that led to this huge demonic trade. There were two churches in the same town. One that was there for a while, and another church that had just received a new reverend. This new reverend was jealous of the other reverend and his church that seemed to have more members (FIRST HUGE ISSUE here). The other huge red flag was that this new reverend saw a demon under every rock, in every busy, in the storms, winds, animals, words, and, for sure, in all that he did not understand! He had a servant girl from Barbados, and two daughters. Well, to make this short, since this guy saw devils and demons in literally everything around him and others, focusing ONLY ON THAT, making that the center of his messages and his job as a "minister" that evil, murderous, accusatory, reality multiplied IN him and around him! That reality literally became the source of his supply and his daughters become possessed by demons, accusatory demons that would bring destruction to that city, and death for so many innocent people; literally destroying families, putting husbands against wives and children against parents, friends against friends, and all this was based IN and because of Fear, Control and Manipulation...PROGRAMMING!

These young daughters of the Reverend would go into fits of possession and in those fits, they would accuse anyone they were "told" to accuse by the spirits that controlled them! This reverend, their father, kept yelling and telling everyone that the devil was in their midst. All he was doing (because, YES, because THAT was his focus) was allowing the evil powers to MULTIPLY and grow in HIM, AND THEY POSSESSED his daughters! The result was that 17 people, God loving people, were killed horribly ... spilling their blood on Cain's trading floor, Apollyon's trading floor, as well as others and, because of that, a false blueprint was now in effect for that city and region.

The first and original city of Salem, as you have read in this book, was a very powerful city that had a portal into the city of Zion, God's realm, and Melchizedach was and still is the King of this city, the City of Peace! This Salem's blueprint was to be a city of REFUGE and PEACE for ALL that would find it, a city that would be an Opened GATE INTO the City of Zion, the city of our God and the FULL supply of THAT city, mirroring THAT, it was to be mirrored and reflected here.

First thing I want you to see is how much chaos and destruction happens when we are operating from the WRONG FOCUS and the wrong perspective. I want you to see and understand the affect it has not only for the person focusing on that, the counterfeit, but the chaos and death it brings around them … to blood lines, generations, and to cities, nations and regions! STOP LOOKING AT demons under every rock! Stop focusing on them, on the counterfeit, and FOCUS ON ADONAI, HIS Kingdom, and ALL that He carries, all that He put inside of your spirit man, IN YOUR ORIGINAL BLUEPRINT!!!

Because of these horrific trades on these demonic trading floors, this city and its region has been operating in the counterfeit blueprint, and, instead of this city being a city of refuge, a city of peace and an open portal into the kingdom realms of El Elyon, it has become the opposite! It became a city of refuge for all that felt cast out and abused by the church, the ones misunderstood by the church and "Christianity", who have been tapping into the counterfeit power, revelation and gates of ascensions.

The other wrong we have been doing is that many well-meaning intercessors how have gone there, went from their position of sitting IN chaos, looking chaos eyeball to eyeball, going to bind demons, all the sprits in that city and area, and coming against principalities. In their assignment, they also went wanting to pull every witch to the side and tell them about Jesus, the One who loves them. Yet, for many of them, that same Jesus was represented by the church in such a horrific light, and even abuse taking place, that the enemy had most of his word done by "Christians in the name of Jesus" and now, these people were totally turned off from God, Jesus, and Christianity!

But, still, good meaning intercessors, being great people themselves, would diligently follow their plan, walking up and down the streets, speaking in tongues, binding every demon. Again, all this was being done SITTNG IN the midst of chaos, from within that chaos completely missing the heart of Adonai and His desire for that city and region!

On our recent trip, Adonai sent us to completely ignore what the enemy was doing in that place, and FROM THE HEART OF THE FATHER, TO SEE the original blueprint for all that was placed in that city and region, engage with THAT and RELEASE THAT! We were to release the opposite of the false, counterfeit, that the enemy had over that city for hundreds of years. I got my AMAZING, INCREDIBLE WARRIOR SONS/KINGS from our Revolution is Here group on Zoom, and together as a UNIT, we ascended INTO the Heart of the Father and we did what He was showing us to do. We entered the Courts of Heaven, repenting for all the bloodshed and the trading done on these demonic floors, asking for forgiveness from the bloodlines affected by these murderous demons and we released THEIR original blueprint and the blessings of The Father. We released the very opposite of what was, up to that point, operating in their family line due to the trauma released. We spoke in tongues as we BLESSED and released the ORIGINAL, which was the OPPOSITE, over that city ... completely the opposite of what the enemy had done in that city! You see, we did not look at the enemy and all he has done and was doing and coming against it all and binding! We completely ignored all of that and focused ONLY ON WHAT THE FATHER WANTED US TO ENGAGE WITH, AND RELEASE ... THE OPPOSITE! We engaged with Melchezidach, King David, and other saints of old. They walked with us in unity releasing THE HEART and LOVE of ADONAI OVER THAT AREA! Do you see how different it is when we engage from His heart, releasing the opposite of the false call, mandate, blueprint? Now, the FULLNESS of THAT original blueprint, the fullness of THAT supply, WILL flow into that city, region, and state. Salem SHALL become the city of OUR GOD and HIS GOVERNMENT!

So, the reason we must first start with us engaging our original blueprint, first, and starting to operate out of that, is because as long as we are fully operating out of the corrupt blueprint, we do not have the full authority to release the original blueprint over any region. Again, remember, the Kingdom of Heaven will not come upon anything that does not look like it. So, we must first, through our lives (meaning: BEGINNING YOUR JOURNEY TO START ...) start operating out of our original blueprint in order to create that shadow, or the landing pad, for the Kingdom of Heaven to see it, and come land on it. Do you understand? Again, unfortunately, the enemy has really used the lack of knowledge and understanding of this process, by good meaning intercessors, and he has used their mouth to reinforce their rule and enlarge their "house".

The next step that is or was done by these good meaning intercessors is that they have not just focused on all that the enemy is doing, or has been doing on his blueprint, and speaking it out, but then there was a spiritual mapping of it! What the enemy was doing was written down by the good meaning intercessors. So, NOW, you also have a DECREE! A decree is a written proclamation that has huge power behind it! A decree is a written, binding document that gives full power to the one that is listed in the decree! For example, in order for you to get your passport, you cannot go and say, "I proclaim that I AM an American citizen because my mom and dad told me so." They will look at you like you have lost your mind and, clearly, they will ask you for your birth certificate ... WHICH IS A WRITTEN PROCLAMATION, A DECREE, to the fact that you indeed are American! A passport is a decree. A marriage certificate IS a decree.

Let's really quickly look at Esther. Remember, though Haman and his sons were hung, and the King gave favor to Esther in such a huge way, the enemies of Esther's people were no longer a threat. However, BECAUSE A DECREE OF DEATH WAS WRITTEN, IT WAS STILL IN EFFECT! So, can we say that there was a CORRUPT BLUEPRINT for ALL of God's people living in that region, that was still in effect? The only way it was able to be stopped was that Esther had to go to the King and ask him to WRITE ANOTHER DECREE, A DECREE OF LIFE...TO SUPERSEDE, TO VOID, AND to TRUMP the previous one.

So, we can see how Esther knew that, though there was victory, her people were STILL under the danger of being killed. They were still under the chaotic, death decree that Haman wrote, and THAT decree was STILL IN POWER, circulating the provinces, RELEASING a mutated blueprint over the Jewish people. So, she realized that she had to do something! She KNEW that GOD HAD A DIFFERENT (HIS ORIGINAL) blueprint for His people, and she had to release THAT! She then wrote ANOTHER DECREE OF LIFE, a decree that spoke of the ORIGINAL BLUEPRINT YHVH HAD FOR HIS PEOPLE, that CANCELED OUT THE DEATH decree, that had been very much still in operation though their enemies, Haman and his evildoers, were dead.

Do YOU UNDERSTAND that you have CREATIVE POWER in your words! What are you PROCLAIMING (meaning: a verbal acknowledgment)? Not only do you have power in your mouth BUT YOUR PEN also carries power! Did you know that? A pen IS a weapon! Are you going to use it as a weapon that GOD can use, or a weapon that the enemy will use?

What do I mean? When you write something down, it becomes a legal, binding, document (aka: a decree). Listen, as intercessors, or really as anyone who is called to pray (either for a nation, region, city, family, church or individual), instead of speaking/PROCLAIMING what we have seen the enemy and all these demons doing, have done, and still trying to do (which means, we are ECHOING and arcing with that particular power of the enemy), OR, even worse, when spiritual mapping happens (meaning when someone puts that into writing, ON PAPER, aka, DECREE/LEGAL BINDING DOCUMENT, all that the enemy has done in this city, or nation, or family, or region, or church or individual, this many generations ago and this principality with this name has been in charge of this gate and it has brought these demons in, that did this and the other...when we write that garbage down), we have JUST REINFORCED, by not only speaking out what they have done, BUT writing it down. We have reestablished those particular powers, with a BINDING, LEGAL, DOCUMENT for them to be able to use which gives them MORE rights and power to continue, or even increase, their hold in that city (region, nation, church, family, individual). Do you understand? WHATEVER YOU LOOK TO, AND FOCUS ON, THAT MULTIPLIES AND THAT BECOMES THAT SOURCE OF YOUR SUPPLY! WHATEVER YOU FOCUS ON, LOOK TO, THAT IS WHAT YOU FEED, THAT IS WHAT GROWS AND MANIFESTS. Do you see?

Then, we try to go to war and fight the very thing that the enemy tricked us to frame and create for him! And we wonder why the situation is now worse off, then it was before we started declaring, proclaiming and decreeing. THIS IS WHY I ONLY SPEAK WHAT GOD SAYS! DO NOT SPEAK, PRAY OR WRITE THE PROBLEM DOWN. SPEAK, PRAY, AND WRITE THE OPPOSITE!

Listen, we do not REALY NEED to know what the enemy has done, or is doing, UNLESS the Lord is desiring to show us! In other words, we do not need to get our cues from the enemy to do the work of the Lord! Again, what we should be doing is getting in our position, in the celestial, IN CHRIST, seated in and with Him, and allow the Father to show us the blueprint and us DECLARING, PROCLAIMING, AND DECREEING THAT ... FRAME UP THAT! Again, like Abraham, go in the celestial and get God's perspective, His original blueprint, and WRITE THAT DOWN...SPEAK THAT OUT, NOT WHAT THE ENEMY IS OR WAS DOING!

Let's review again. Your blueprint is your original plan, design or representation that carries the sound and the frequency of the government and the voice of Yahweh, that He intertwined, mingled, and braided into your spirit man, when you were still in Him, before the foundations of the world. Inside of THAT, your original blueprint is your destiny scroll(s).

Your destiny scroll is your PURPOSE, your fate, your unique call. YOUR GIFTINGS ARE ATTACHED TO YOUR DESTINY SCROLL(S). So, your destiny scroll is a scroll with a seal on it, that is inside your original blueprint, which is inside your spirit man. You can NOT walk out your TRUE original "CALL", your TRUE destiny scroll, if you are not operating out of your original blueprint! You see, our true destiny scroll IS ONLY FOUND INSIDE OUR ORIGINAL BLUEPRINT so if we do not operate out of THAT, we are not truly walking out our original destiny scroll! That is why there is so much jealousy and competition in the body of Christ ... because we don't really know who we are, so we are trying to have our "call"/our destiny be like Tom, Joe, or Henry and we try to copy them, and we get jealous that they are doing a better job than what we think we are doing ... and this is again because we are walking out a counterfeit destiny scroll out of a mutated blueprint! Do you understand?

We're supposed to all be working for the same kingdom!! It's not my little ministry and your little ministry, copying your style, your words, your encounters, your messages, because I don't know what I really am and now, I am jealous because you have more people than I do. Now, I even feel the need to tear you down because somehow that makes me think I look better. OH MY GOSH...NOT IS NOT WHAT SHOULD BE HAPPENING! We are all supposed to reflect the facets of our original blueprint, and walking our our original destiny scrolls, UNITED, to LIFT HIM UP and point people to HIM and His Kingdom and to who He says that they are, and START TAKING CARE OF BUSINESS IN UNITY, toppling over the kingdom in darkness!!!!

I know I am repeating myself again, but I want to make sure you fully understand. If you don't know what YOUR original blueprint is, there's no way you can walk YOUR destiny.

Let's say you are dealing with a bad medical report. That report is speaking a mutated blueprint and attached to that is a mutated destiny. Example: you are NOT a diabetic, which would be a mutated blueprint, and you will NOT have to rely on and continue to take shots of insulin, which is a mutated, corrupt, destiny! Do you understand?

Although you need to follow the wisdom of your doctor, when dealing with the spirit realm, you always listen to the leading of The Father. What you have to do is, now that you've heard the doctor's report, and are heeding the doctor's advice (until, in the natural, there is a change in that report), is to step OUT of that reality, in and THROUGH THE DOOR OF the Kingdom of God, which, remember, is in YOU! Step in and through THAT reality, which again, is a portal into the Kingdom of Heaven and, even more, INTO THE HEART OF ADONAI! You do all this BY FAITH, engaging your desire, through your God given imagination, Now, LOOK, SEEK, sense the Father or Jesus there. Do NOT discount ANYTHING or do not second guess ... just trust and believe, by faith! Engage all of your senses and, again, by faith, just tell Him, "Show me, Daddy, show me what YOU say! Show me my original blueprint! I know it is not what the doctor just told me. It is not what the bank statement just showed me. It is not what these court papers tell me. It is not what that person says about me ... show me, Daddy." What do you hear, or sense that you see, or sense that you feel? Write THAT down and DECLARE THAT, out of the Kingdom of Heaven OVER whatever counterfeit blueprint and destiny you received!

Now, you may not see anything shifting or changing, however you keep doing it until you see the change coming! You be like that bulldog that grabs something and does not let go! Remember, the Kingdom of God suffers violence, BUT the violent TAKE IT BY FORCE!

Remember, it's all about DNA! The blueprint carries the government of God, the frequency of God, the voice of God and the original DNA, HIS DNA, that God put inside your spirit man when you were IN Him, in the very beginning.

Let me share with you a period of my life where I know that it is a time in my life where the enemy hates that he tried to mess with me, my God given blueprint, and my destiny that I was supposed to walk out in that period of time. It was late spring of 2013, and I just had my baby boy, our last one. I was in Florida, scheduled to teach two weeks at a school of the supernatural. Steve, my hubby, went to Romania because his father was not doing well. So, I stayed with my two younger babies with my parents who lived in South Florida. Two days before I was supposed to start the school, oh my goodness, I felt this pain that, unfortunately, I was very familiar with because of my past history of kidney stones. The pain of kidney stones is quite insane, so I knew that I did NOT have time for this; ESPECIALLY because I had to start the school! I was like, "Oh, Lord. NO NO NO NOOOO...this is NOT happening and definitely NOT NOW! Steve is out of the country. I am in Florida with my babies … my three-month-old and my four-year-old … and I have to prepare! NO WAY!" I tell you...had the enemy known what the Lord was going to do with me, in the midst of that pain, he would've never touched me!!!

YHVH's catapulting of me in these higher realms and dimensions where He started to unveil His mysteries, teaching me in TANGIBLE ways, STARTED DURING THAT ATTACK on my physical body in the midst of that insane pain. He started unfolding all these things, literally, night after night, day after day, week after week, as He was teaching me what it really means to step into MY POSITION IN HIM. He was showing me how I can STEP OUT OF THE DOOR OF MY REALITY, INTO AND THROUGH THE DOOR OF HIS REALITY, HIS DIMENSION, INTO THE CELESTIAL, where I was to be seated. From there, He started teaching me every night, throughout the night, and in the morning, He had me write it all down and He would say, "Now, Corina, this is what you are teaching tonight at the school." For three months, I did have not sleep at all! In the evening, I went to teach and minister. I was teaching with two stents in my kidneys, bleeding out, as I was standing on my feet (still in my heels … if you know me, you've laughed right there) for hours, pouring out ALL He put in me the night before. I was SEEING people TRULY UNDERSTANDING WHO THEY WERE, TAKING THEM TO HEAVEN as THEY WERE SEEING JESUS FOR THE VERY FIRST TIME. In those encounters, Jesus was showing them what He knew they needed to see in order for them to be set free from the bondages they were bound in, in that time and season! Demons would literally leave people, screaming, without anyone laying hands on them. It is NOT about anyone laying hands on, really, it is about YOU and me SEEING Jesus, seeing God the Father, SEEING the original blueprint and letting ALL OF THAT, your original blueprint and my original blueprint "LAY HANDS" on, if you will, and let IT FIGHT ON YOUR BEHALF and on my behalf! That is how we are to fight...from our TRUE position IN HIM!

You guys, I am no longer in a place where I just want to see what is in the hand of God, I am not any longer in a place where I just want to stop at seeing His face, as AMAZING AS THAT IS! I do not want to stop until I learn to LIVE out of the chambers of His heart, and mirror THAT, into everything and everywhere!

ARE YOU A STAR - WALKER?

One night, after teaching and ministering, arriving back home till about 2:00 in the morning, I lay in bed just continuing to worship the Father. I was worshipping Him with every fiber of my being in pure, childlike love and adoration, feeling as if my heart would explode with such intense love for Him! All of a sudden, this tangible cloud fills the room. It was a very thick cloud above my head, and it was so present and visible, that it covered the entire ceiling of the room, extending down, halfway in the room. There was no more ceiling. What now replaced it was this thick, soft looking, very light, light blue cloud that, again, extended almost halfway in the room, from the ceiling. As my hands were lifted in worship, this thick cloud came down even more, covering my hand and half of my arms and, all of a sudden, they disappeared in the cloud! As I would bring them back down, they reappeared and as I was putting them back up in the cloud, they would disappear again! This cloud was now just above my head, but in the entire room.

So, I looked up, and oh my goodness, my hands were gone in that beautiful, cloud of glory that was now over me. I would bring them down, out of the cloud, and there they were I would put them back up, and they again disappeared!

As you can imagine, I was in awe! I could not believe my eyes! The entire atmosphere of the room was electric with His thick, tangible glory and His tangible love, so much so that every cell of my being was vibrating in response and all I could do is pour my love out to Him, as tears streamed down my face, feeling His love wrapping every ounce of my being, my spirit, soul and body.

All of a sudden, I heard Him say to me, "Corina, look around the room." You guys, EVERYTHING in that room was in movement! Every ounce of that room ... the walls, the furniture, the paintings on the wall, the pictures on the furniture, the silk plants in the room, everything was in movement! It's as if He stripped away everything of this "natural" reality and I was able to see the very subatomic particles, their movement. I saw these particles of EVERYTHING in that room moving so very fast, kinda like millions and millions of tiny dots, moving at extreme speed, in different directions. Then, I saw them shift and create a wave like pattern, again moving at incredible speed.

As I was watching this in awe, I heard the Father say, "Corina, now, all you have to do is walk through it! Because what you are carrying inside your DNA is a much higher frequency, the highest frequency, it is the ultimate creatIVE LIGHT that created all that you see, all that is in creaTED light, all you need to do is get up and go walk through the wall!" I, however, could absolutely not move! I was in such a place of His pure glory and presence, that I literally could not move, but saturate in that great love, absorb it, and cry as I poured my love upon my Father.

Let me share with you another incredible testimony that involves my little girl, Majesty, who was only four years old, at that time. She was partaking in almost all of these experiences, as she was sleeping with me, and many times she would fall asleep in the middle of one of these powerful encounters that she would also have.

Remember, I have been telling the Lord that I would absolutely teach anything that He wanted me to teach, however, I would never teach from head knowledge, only experiential knowledge. Two days after the incredible experience I mentioned above, Yeshuah took me deeper into the unveiling of the next layer of the mysteries found in His DNA, the power and frequency it carries, and that if we can just realize that, engage with THAT, and operate out of His DNA that is supposed to be UNLOCKED from within our spirit man, death would have NO POWER OVER US, NOTHING WOULD and, truly then, no weapons formed against us WOULD EVER PROSPER, because EVERYTHING of a lower frequency MUST BOW ITS KNEE TO THE AUTHORITY AND POWER THAT IS IN HIS DNA!

So, he began to teach me even more about the difference between creaTIVE light and creaTED light and that the creaTIVE light carries the ultimate power...ultimate wave and particle, frequency, energy, sound...that created ALL that is in the creaTED light, that also consists of wave and particle, of the light that it carries. So, everything that you see on the earth and in the cosmos is made up of the waves and particles of creatED light.

However, in our original DNA, the light that bursts forth is HIS creaTIVE light because as HE IS NOW, SO ARE WE...IN THIS WORLD! So that means, ALL that He does, creates, manifests, we should do as well...THAT IS WHAT IS WRITTEN IN OUR ORIGINAL BLUEPRINT!

On this hot Florida afternoon, I was in the kitchen, just finished giving our little baby boy, Justice, a bath. Majesty was playing with her toys in the room where we were sleeping, which had a huge armoire with a heavy TV, a TV box, four drawers full of clothes, and a big, heavy, clay vase on top of the armoire with large silk flowers. I had just wrapped Justice up in a towel when, all of a sudden, I heard this big crash coming from the back room, and I froze for a few seconds. I immediately knew what happened. I just knew that the armoire fell. Fear gripped me as my mind immediately went to the worst possible outcome … did the armoire fall on Majesty? Now, Majesty was a very tiny four-year-old and I feared the worst if indeed that huge furniture piece fell on her!

As my mind is racing full of anxiety and panic, honestly, fearing the worst, trying to give Justice, to my mom or dad so I can run and find Majesty, Majesty runs into the kitchen, saying, "Mommy, mommy, I'm okay! It fell on me, but I am OK!" As my mind was still going ten thousand miles a second, realizing that clearly, a miracle just took place! She quickly proceeded to tell me that she was trying to reach for her toy, that somehow was on top of the armoire, so she climbed up in it, trying to reach the toy, and the armoire fell! Immediately, I knew that there was a supernatural intervention. An angel must have literally grabbed her, and thrown her to the side, out of the way of the armoire as it came crashing down because there is no way she would have had time to climb down and jump to the side of it before it came crashing down. Had it fallen on her; she would not have been here today.

After things calmed down and I put Justice to sleep, I brought her to me and began to ask her for details. "Baby, tell me what happened". She said, "Mommy, it fell on me but I'm okay". Thinking that, clearly, she is not understanding my question, I asked her again. "Baby, did an angel grab you and push you to the side before the furniture fell?" "No, mommy. It fell on me but, you see, I am ok"! She proceeded to tell me this for the second time with a little more emphasis behind her explanation. I was positive that she just did not comprehend the severity of the reality that IF that armoire fell on her, she would have been in very bad shape, so I feel that I have to explain it to her a bit clearer, so that she could tell me the truth of what happened. In my mind, she clearly did not understand my question. So, I asked her for the third time. "No, honey, if that would have fallen on you, you would have been extremely hurt so it could not have fallen on you. What happened?" She put her little hands on her waist, with a firm conviction and said, "No, mommy, it fell on me, but I got out through the hole!" Oh, my goodness, I thought, what hole? There was no hole!

Immediately, the Lord spoke very loud and clear to me and said, "Did you not ask me and say to me that you want to experience my power in such a manner before you go teach it? The very FREQUENCY - sound, vibration, energy source, power and the authority of my DNA that is in her came forth, and that lower frequency that is in the molecules in that armoire, recognized what is in her, submitted to THAT, and made a hole for her to go through it!"

Do you understand what really lives IN you? Oh, if you would just recognize it, and engage with it. When you recognize it and you engage with it, THAT power of Adonai that is at the core of your spirit man, that should be pulsating through every cell of your body, woven in your original DNA, carries resurrection LIFE and resurrection POWER. Therefore, NOTHING can touch you ... no weapons formed against you can succeed because GREATER IS HE that is in YOU than anything that is out there, than any other frequency/sound, vibration, energy, power and authority!

Again, this huge God shift happened in me, and to me, when the enemy tried to bring this huge attack against my body. He thought he would stop me from doing my assignment, teaching a school of the supernatural, BUT GOD! Had the enemy known how the Lord was going to use what he meant for bad, for a complete and total shift IN me, and how this would reflect Adonai's glory, he would have never tried to mess with me! Let me, though, say this ... I STILL had a CHOICE ... To stay in bed, wallow in the pain, feel sorry for myself, and be angry at God for allowing such an attack ... allowing surgery, medical bills, and so on ... Would the shift have happened to me and ALL that it brought? Absolutely not. Because, though He had these things prepared for me, it was MY CHOICE to step in it or not. Do not let the fullness of His plans for you pass you by! It is your choice to see them and step into them!

Now, let's again go back to Abraham. So, you guys, in a sense, Abraham was a star-walker. He walked among the stars. In the Bible, it says that God told him, "Look toward the stars." Do you know what towards means? It means to look ahead of you. It does not mean "stretch your head up as high as you can and look UP at the stars!" No. It means that the stars are in front of you so, look ahead of you, look INTO the light that they give. Do you see the difference? In another translation it says to "TELL the stars if you can count them." So, Abraham was IN the light given by the stars. He was WALKING AMONG the stars! WOW!

Enoch was also a star-walker. God has never stopped looking for star-walkers because we are to go IN (the Kingdom of God that is IN our spirit man) and THROUGH (the veil that was already torn, waiting for you to walk through it, into the Kingdom of Heaven) and UP (in our position) IN heavenly places (which also includes to walk among the stars)! That is where you find your TRUE, ORIGINAL blueprint; not sitting on the earth, in your carnal temple, in the midst of chaos ... NO! Go IN, THROUGH, and UP. SEE YOUR BLUEPRINT. Engage it AND WALK OUT YOUR DESTINY SCROLL ... OUT OF YOUR ORIGINAL BLUEPRINT!

These messages are for people who are not afraid to go there. Are you one of those radical, peculiar ones? God HAS NEVER, ever, stopped looking for star-walkers. ARE YOU A STAR-WALKER?

Keep in mind that fear will keep you bound to the terrestrial. Fear of "the new", fear of stepping outside the box or tradition and religion, fear of what your pastor, your friends, and family will say, fear of ... "is this really you, God, or a demon trying to trick me?" Fear, fear, fear! God has never, will NOT EVER, operate in, with, or through fear! So, if you feel fear, that is your clear indication that it is the enemy trying to STOP YOU from stepping in the NEXT level of you understanding your identity and learning how to operate out of it by engaging your original blueprint. He's trying to stop you from going from your last "step of glory" onto the NEXT "step of glory"! Remember, we are to go FROM glory TO glory, which means, I MUST MOVE...NOT STAY STUCK at the last move of God, the glory of the past ... not stay stuck in tradition of my faith BUT move into the NEXT layer and level of revelation and go from glory to glory!

Therefore, God positioned Abraham up there to show us a pattern God always uses patterns. Why? Because God uses patterns to give us an image of what He wants to build on the earth AND what He wants to do in the heavens.

Let's look at Colossians 1:13, 16,20, 25-26 AMP.
v.13 The Father has (past tense, already did it) delivered and drawn us to Himself. (Where is He? In heavenly places? So, He has already drawn us to Himself) out of the control and the dominion of darkness and HAS transferred us INTO the kingdom the son. v16. For it was in Him that ALL things were created in the heavens and on the earth and under the earth...

"Under the earth" does not just mean in the core of the earth, but it means that and more! It also means in the cosmos ... because the earth is in the cosmos, held together by dark matter and dark energy. Why? Because, like I said at the very beginning, God is a multidimensional God and His language is a multidimensional language that does not just have one meaning, understanding, application, or interpretation. However deep you want to go in His word, which remember, are LIVING BEINGS, that is how deep these living beings will take you in! ... things seen and things unseen, whether thrones, dominions, rulers or authorities; all things were created and EXIST THROUGH HIM and IN and for Him!

Watch! v.20 "And God purposed that THROUGH (by the service of the intervention of) Him [The Son] ALL things should be completely reconciled back to Himself, whether on earth or in heaven, as through Him, [the Father] made peace by means of the blood of His cross.

What is the cross for? Not JUST for salvation! That is the VERY BEGINNING. It is NOT the end-all! It starts with the cross! The cross is also your entry point, the portal for you to enter and go through it, into the fullness that Jesus gave you access to have and take back all that Adam lost by agreeing with the trade! What is the blood for? It is to give you the ability to engage in the ORIGINAL record of the DNA of Yeshua, so that it can recreate in YOU what you were in the beginning, when you were IN THE FATHER, before the foundations of this word, before the unraveling that took place in the Adam's DNA.

So, God purposed it that, through the blood and the cross, all things should be completely reconciled ... all things seen AND unseen. Do we think He's only talking about earth? No, ALL of creation ... which means every planet, every star that is in every dimension, every multiverse, every time frame...ALL things seen AND unseen. Cosmologists are saying that for every grain of sand on the earth, there is an earth - like planets that can sustain life, and this is only in the little corner of our universe that they can actually see! Can you imagine? ALL of that is looking to US ... to awaken out of our spiritual amnesia and realize who we are, whose we are and the power, authority, AND RESPONSIBILITY WE HAVE, and for us to take dominion over the earth, THROUGH LOVE, cleanse the heavens (ALL of it), and bring the restoration of El Elyon in ALL! Does it happen by us standing here on the earth in the midst of chaos, trying to pull heaven down by saying what we THINK heaven is saying, and releasing what we THINK God is wanting to release, because the Religious Spirits have used Fear, to tell us that we can't go IN, THROUGH and UP? God is STILL looking for STAR-WALKERS who will not be afraid to GO, see, and RELEASE HIS Blueprint! 200 BILLION galaxies with one BILLION - TRILLION STARS are waiting FOR YOU!!!! And this is just what is visible in our little corner of the universe!

Listen, God always uses people to set a precedent so that God can bring men into a position of responsibilities into the heavenlies, first, and THEN, ON THE EARTH! It starts in Heaven first. That is where your training happens! You guys, again, sitting in the middle of chaos trying to pull down heaven DOES NOT WORK! As I have said before, we have to remember that He will not come upon anything that doesn't look like Him. Chaos does not look like Him! He comes where He sees a shadow of Himself, or His kingdom. Jesus taught us about this… "Your Kingdom come, Your will be done, on earth, AS IT IS IN HEAVEN!" As you can see, it starts from Heaven … so, then, earth takes on the reflection OF HEAVEN. We need to learn what our position is from heaven. We need to get our strategy and what needs to happen on earth and in ALL of creation from Heaven and then, we release it on earth. Earth then shall mirror the Kingdom of Heaven and His government because we are supposed to be living in Heaven and existing here on the earth. So, we REFLECT the place we are LIVING IN and FROM (Heaven) into the place where we exist (earth).

If you want to really display His authority in ALL creation like you are really supposed to, THEN, you have to learn to go UP AND, after, reflect down before you can go, to and fro. Meaning, you cannot release His authority across the cosmos and in all creation or, in other words, going to and fro, BEFORE you learn to go IN, THROUGH, UP and THEN, down.

When you understand your position … when you understand that you have access to get your original blueprint, the blueprint of God, and ALL that it carries with it, and you RELEASE THAT, EVERYTHING that is around you, everything, even at a subatomic particle level, that is around you will shift and change! Why? Because you have just released the frequency, which is the very sound, vibration, voice of the full authority and power of El Elyon, God MOST HIGH, into your atmosphere! Therefore, everything that is in that atmosphere will shift and take on the image of your original blueprint, God's blueprint! You have JUST BECOME THE GATE THAT YOU REALLY ARE supposed to be, the portal that you really are supposed to be, AND OUT OF YOUR GATE, HIS REFLECTION OF WHO YOU REALLY WERE IN HIM before the foundations of the earth WILL FLOW OUT AND TRANSFORM THE MOLECULAR STRUCTURE IN YOU, all that is around you, and all the chaos that has been operating will be transformed into what YOUR ORIGINAL BLUEPRINT says, for this time, and this season! THIS IS HOW WE WAR!

Let's look at David a bit. The Bible says that David went into the wilderness driven by Saul and it states that 300 men gathered to him who were outcasts in Israel. Do you know why they were called outcasts? Because they were of a different seed line! What was different about them?

We see in 2 Samuel 23:8-39 and in 1 Chronicles 11:22, a clear picture of why these men were so different. It says that one of them killed 400 men, and another one killed 800 men. These men had incredible powers, unlike a normal human. We read about these men, who were now seen as outcasts, in Genesis 6. It says that these men were the children that were born to the daughters of man, that were half human, half sons of God, or Watchers. They become known as the Nephilims, the mighty men who were of old, men of renown. So, because they were of a mixed, wrong seed-line, they became the outcasts in Israel.

However, here is the insight of one that worked FROM HEAVEN'S position, tapping into the CELESTIAL, bringing the blueprint of God, into the terrestrial! Listen, David was not just out there in the fields playing his harp and singing all day long. NO! David was ACTUALLY GOING SOMEWHERE WITH, AND IN, GOD! The Bible says that though David did a lot of "crappy" things, God loved him so very much! Why? It says that David was AFTER the

HEART OF GOD! He completely pursued the heart of God with everything that he had in him! When you pursue something with all of your might, and if you don't give up, you WILL OBTAIN that which you have pursued and desired. Therefore, David went after the heart of God so much, with everything he had in him, (you guys, IT IS ALL ABOUT ... RELATIONSHIP, RELATIONSHIP, RELATIONSHIP), not stopping at anything, no matter what the cost, until he ACTUALLY, NOT ONLY FOUND THE HEART OF GOD, BUT, ALSO, WENT IN the heart of God AND LEARNED HOW TO LIVE HIS LIFE FROM WITHIN HEART OF GOD! As he did that, David actually stepped into the TIMELINE of God. Meaning, David stepped OUTSIDE OF HIS TIMELINE, ALL his limitations, all that held him bound to the chaotic atmosphere that was around him, binding him to THAT REALITY, that space and time, and all that was encompassed in there. Living from the heart of God, David stepped OUTSIDE OF ALL OF THAT, and into the timeline that consists of the REALITY that Adonai had for him, the reality of what that great I AM THAT I AM had for him, which was found in his future, in the AGE TO COME!

You see, in the Hebrew mindset and understanding of the Word of YHVH is that where you begin, you must end up ... meaning, your beginning MUST mirror your end though there is no end, only a future. (More on this in a bit). Your future then, MUST mirror your beginning! In this manner, really there IS NO END because this is a never-ending circle that consists of your beginning mirroring your future, and your future mirroring your beginning! Therefore, there is a complete circle! So, who you were when you were in the Father, before the foundations of the world were created, and WHAT you carried (meaning, the FULLNESS of what you were and the FULLNESS of what you carried ... aka your original blueprint) IS ALWAYS MIRRORING WHO YOU ARE IN THE FUTURE. That IS YOUR TRUE REALITY!

Let's go back to David. So, because now, David lived out of the timeline of God, that is how he saw his future! That is how he knew there was a Holy Spirit and he RECEIVED IT 400 years BEFORE THE HOLY SPIRIT WAS RELEASED! Remember, he cried out to the Lord and said, "Do not take Your Holy Spirit from me!" That is how David knew, because he SAW his original blueprint and that he indeed WAS going to be king, and NOTHING would stop him from walking out this part of his destiny scroll. As he was walking THAT OUT of his original blueprint! That is also how David knew that, though the lion and the bear come after him, they would not kill him because he KNEW and SAW his original blueprint that he was going to be king! That is how he knew that no matter what Saul would try, all the traps, all the plans Saul had to kill him, he would not succeed because, David SAW HIS BLUEPRINT ... DAVID SAW HIS FUTURE!

Not only did David SEE his future, but DAVID LIVED HIS PRESENT REALITY OUT OF THE REALITY OF THE AGE TO COME, OUT OF THE REALITY OF HIS ORIGINAL BLUEPRINT, OUT OF THE REALITY OF HIS FUTURE! So, as David learned to LIVE OUT OF THE HEART OF GOD THE MOST INTIMATE PLACE OF GOD (RELATIONSHIP), DAVID PULLED HIS FUTURE INTO HIS PRESENT UNTIL HIS CURRENT CHAOTIC REALITY, AND ALL ITS VOICES, HAD TO BOW ITS KNEE AND SUBMIT TO THE FUTURE AND THE REALITY THAT GOD HAD FOR HIM!

IF YOU KNOW YOUR FUTURE, YOUR PRESENT CANNOT KILL YOU!

Therefore, because now, the very atmosphere where David was EXISTING (in the cave) was taking on the image and reflection of him living from the heart of God and God's original blueprint which carries the frequency, the voice, the power, the authority, the responsibility, the government, and the REALITY of GOD, it affected everyone in that cave MEANING, ALL OF THESE 400 MEN'S MUTATED BLUEPRINTS WERE AND IT TRANSFORMED INTO WHAT THE ORIGINAL BLUEPRINT OF EL ELYON SAID THAT THEY ARE TO BE! NO LONGER OUTCASTS, BUT RIGHTEOUS, JUDGES IN ISRAEL! How do we know that? Because it says that when David became king in Israel, they all became JUDGES! Let's break it down a bit more. This means that the fullness of what they were FRAMED IN got so changed by the glory that overshadowed and flowed out of David being in his position, that it CHANGED their CHAOTIC DNA into the original blueprint and desire of God!

Because there was one man that understood the principle of God, one man that entered the heart of God, it not only transformed him but a people's group, AND A NATION! What can God do with a mature son who allows the process of maturity to teach him/her who they are, that will then be presented to Adonai, ready to be anointed as kings, out of their position of mature sons; that learn how to enter into the heart ... His heart, live out of His heart and RELEASE HIS ORIGINAL BLUEPRINT INTO ALL OF CREATION TO EVERY BEING, IN EVERY PLANET AND STAR SYSTEM, IN EVERY DIMENSION, IN EVERY MULTIVERSE, EVERY TIMELINE, IN THE COSMOS, INSIDE THE EARTH AND ALL OVER THE EARTH? WHAT DO YOU THINK WILL HAPPEN WHEN HE CAN FIND THESE SONS ... THESE ELECT ONES, THESE PECULIAR ONES, THAT WILL BE LIKE DAVID, TO STOP AT NOTHING UNTIL THEY RELEASE THE FULLNESS OF THE ORIGINAL BLUEPRINT OF EL ELYON, ADONAI, OF EL ROI, OF EL SHADDAI, EMANUEL, OF YHVH, YEHOVA RAPHA, YEHOVAH SHAM, YEHOVAH GMOLAH, YEHOVAH JIREH, YEHOVAH TSABAOTH? ARE YOU ONE OF THESE? IF SO, THIS...IS... HOW ...YOU...WAR!

Before we go on, this point is so important, and I want to make sure you get it so I will say it again, maybe breaking it down a bit more. You see, God wants to bring everything back to completion. ALL the unraveling that the enemy did ... leaving loose, mutated DNA lines, leaving "loose ends" disconnections that have brought about a disconnection in you from your TRUE identity, disconnected from the fullness of your heavenly family and all that it entails; and bound you to the chaotic reality that has limited you to it, and imprisoned you to its limitations and laws that are NOT part of your original blueprint! God wants to bring all that consists of who you are BACK in unity, to connect it all back to Him, and to your original blueprint.

That is why it's so important that you SEE your original blueprint and who you were created to be before He created anything, before He created time and space, and when you see that, and engage in it, releasing THAT into your current reality, let me tell you something ... it's going to shift your present reality INTO WHO YOU SEE that you are in YOUR AGE TO COME, which is YOUR FUTURE which, again, looks like your beginning, AND ALL OF THE ABILITIES THAT COMES WITH THAT ... YOUR PRESENT WILL NO LONGER LOOK LIKE THE CHAOTIC REALITY, BUT YOUR PRESENT WILL LOOK LIKE YOUR FUTURE, WHICH LOOKS LIKE YOUR BEGINNING! DO YOU UNDERSTAND? REMEMBER, IF YOU KNOW YOUR FUTURE AND YOU PULL IT IN YOUR PRESENT (you have a choice here, again), YOUR PRESENT CAN NOT KILL YOU BECAUSE IT TAKES ON THE REFLECTIONS OF WHO YOU ARE IN THE FATHER...IT TAKES ON THE REFLECTION OF YOUR ORIGINAL BLUEPRINT!

Remember, YOUR CHOICE CHOOSES YOU!

Whatever's going on in your life. you have the ability to change! Remember what the Bible says in Colossians 3:2 TPT... "FEAST (to chew or meditate) yourself on ALL treasures of heavenly realms and FILL your thoughts (meditate, IMAGINE, engage your God given imagination) with heavenly realities and NOT on the distractions of this world."

What do you do when you feast? You SIT DOWN so you can properly eat all types of yummy foods. In this verse, you feast on ALL, NOT SOME, BUT ALL! It's YOUR CHOICE of how much you want to feast on, what treasures of THAT realm you want to enjoy. But, here, we are clearly told that we can feast on ALL TREASURES OF HEAVENLY REALMS! Now, this does not mean standing up like you would eat fast food! So, you have to SIT! KEY! For we ARE SEATED IN HEAVENLY PLACES IN God the Father with Christ Jesus, FAR ABOVE ALL powers, principalities, demonic forces, evil spirits and so on. So, SITTING has to do with GETTING YOUR TOUCHES IN YOUR POSITION! You canNOT feast on Heavenly treasures if you DON'T SIT UP THERE! YOU ARE NOT TO SIT HERE in chaos! Do you see?

All you have to do is get yourself in that position, in the Celestial, NOT terrestrial, and allow the Lord to show you your blueprint, and release THAT no matter what your present circumstances look like! DO IT BY FAITH!

We don't have to fight the devil eyeball to eyeball. Are you starting to understand what warfare really means? Warfare means that you get in your position IN GOD, in His heart, which is the most INTIMATE PLACE OF WHO HE IS ... it's THE CORE of who He is FAR ABOVE ... outside of their reach because you are not only in God but IN HIS HEART, at the very center of His being! Everything that is not of God (and all its powers including death, sickness, disease, mortality ... and all that is encapsulated in the kingdom in darkness including linear time and space) IS actually enclosed in a capsule that El Elyon holds in the palm of His hand!

So, then, ALL you have to do is keep your eyes fixed on the RIGHT BLUEPRINT that is found in and through the heart of God, and not on the things of this world and this chaotic reality but on the things that we see from our position seated in Him. Then, RELEASE what you see BY FAITH, or what you SENSE that you SEE that is part of your blueprint! As you do that, the SOUND that you are releasing by faith that comes from your original blueprint will IMPOSE ITSELF ON THE EARTH, in the chaotic reality and atmosphere, and it will REFRAME THE CHAOTIC BLUEPRINT UNTIL that chaotic blueprint will take on the form of the Heavenly blueprint! Let me put it in a very simple strategy ... RELEASE THE OPPOSITE OF WHAT

YOU ARE SEEING IN YOUR FALSE, CHAOTIC, REALITY! GOD ALWAYS says, and has, the opposite of all that the enemy is trying to do or say ... So, again, RELEASE THE OPPOSITE OF WHAT YOU SEE AND HEAR the enemy trying to do in your life, in your family, in your city, in your church, in your region, in your nation, in the earth, under the earth, and in ALL creation! IGNORE

ALL that you see the enemy doing, saying, acting, and RELEASE THE OPPOSITE because your blueprint ALWAYS SPEAKS the opposite of what the enemy is saying and doing. Remember, he canNOT tell the truth! Therefore, all that he says ARE LIES! Whatever you are dealing with ... sickness, disunity, lack, fear, hopelessness, craziness, rebellion, ... no matter what, SPEAK THE OPPOSITE!

Why is the blueprint of God so important for us to understand, to engage it and to release it? Because, in the beginning, God established government to rule! His blueprint CARRIES HIS GOVERNMENT! That is why, IN THE CELESTIAL arena, when we look at the blueprint, we will find government! His government MUST be established IN EVERYTHING from us as individuals to nations to the multiverse, but it must be established from UP THERE!

So, when we bring the blueprint of Heaven, THAT government gets IMPOSED upon EVERYTHING, until the government of the earthly arena, or the cosmos, or a family, or an individual, is superseded and taken over by the government of our God.

If you stand down here, you will hear His voice SHROUDED in chaos. Just relying on hearing Him is not enough! You see, not only will His voice be shrouded in the chaos that is around you, but you will hear His voice through all the bent perspectives that you have about who He really is and who you really are to Him! In other words, His voice will be shrouded in the chaotic atmosphere that is around you and in you! That is why it is very important that we, now, learn to go IN (inside our spirit man where the Kingdom of God is) that gives us free access to go THROUGH (the veil/the portal of the Kingdom of Heaven that is a close to you as the air that you breathe, that is at hand) and UP in our position, seated far above ALL, to actually SEE the voice that is speaking!

You guys, this means that there is a TRADE that is required of you! I will only touch on this a bit here but, for you to get the full understanding on this subject, you can find it in my previous book called, Unveiling the Trading Floors & Stepping into the Order of

Melchizedek. What do I mean by "it requires a trade from you"? Trade with YOUR TIME in order to build that close relationship with Him. It takes time to build a relationship, does it not? Why do we feel like we can just give him crumbs of our time and somehow that is enough? Again, it's all about your CHOICE and my CHOICE...how bad do I want to step into ALL that He gave me access to have?

Then, we may need to trade on the intent and desires of our heart, for the intent and the desires of His heart. What He wants for you is so much greater than what you can want for yourself! His thoughts and intents are so much higher for you, more than you can think or imagine, but you have to give up yours, or trade yours, for His! Trade with every part of your being that which is not aligned with His heart and His best for you! If your eyes are engaging in something that is going to have legal right over you and your bloodline, you must trade that for His eyes, that you see like He sees, that you look at things that He would look at because, remember whatever you look to multiplies and THAT becomes the source of your supply. This right here is a trade of yourself as a living sacrifice ... every part of you for every part of Him! Again, I have written much more on this subject in my previous book that I have mentioned above.

Then, there is a trade that you are to make for your lack of faith for His faithfulness. Your fear for His love, your weakness and unbelief for His strength and trust. So, as you can see, when you are with Him, He will take away the old IF you CHOOSE to trade it with Him and will give you HIS BEST! ALL that is found in your original blueprint IS the TRADE that He has for you...of your old, carnal, mutated, limited, human bound reality for HIS REALITY which says that "I CAN DO ALL things with Christ, for as He is NOW... (how does Jesus look like now?????) so AM I, IN THIS WORLD...NOT when I die!" And these are just TWO scriptures ONLY!

As you TRADE with Him, and you engage in your original blueprint you WILL THEN become the VOICE of His Truth, releasing His original blueprint, onto the earth, onto the Kingdom of the Earth, REFRAMING what has been birth in chaos INTO THE

IMAGE of HIS GOVERNMENT and the SOUND OF HIS BLUEPRINT!

Again, understand that OUR function MUST BE...HEAVEN TO EARTH, NOT earth to Heaven! Listen, anyone that tells you that what you are doing is wrong and demonic, witchcraft, IS the voice of the enemy speaking THROUGH CHAOS, speaking THROUGH the sound - frequency of the Tower of Babel telling you that, "You cannot have something greater and more powerful than I have. You cannot go through that gate ... because I am going to stand in as a gatekeeper and try to stop you!" That, my friend, is part of what a principality does! You, again, have a choice! Are you going to listen to that voice, or ignore it and go in your position and do what the Father tells you to do?

When God opened up this truth for Abraham to SEE ... THIS TRUTH, then, dictated his behavior! When Abraham saw that truth of the SUPPLY of Heaven, as he was SITTING and FEASTING in the arena of THAT REALITY, THAT reality, then, began to dictate his every action and his behavior. That reality and arena is also where I believe Abraham met Melchizedek...and KNEW who he was...understanding his position. That is why, when he encountered Melchizedek on the earth, he KNEW that he had an opportunity to trade INTO the title of his name, and into the position that was established in Melchezedek's name. Abraham also understood, as I mentioned in the beginning of this book, that when he was trading with Melchizedek, he was not only for himself but FOR ALL of his future generations!

Because Abraham set in, and feasted on, the celestial arena of God, he was able to walk in the FULL restoration of life that he saw God had for him, no matter what his natural body said! He SAW ALL the children that he was going to have ... so many that he was not able to count them. Therefore, THAT became his reality, and THAT reality superseded the false reality of his natural body and IT TRANSFORMED HIM ... ACCORDING TO GOD'S BLUEPRINT! Let me say it again. Because the blueprint found in the celestial IS HIS TRUTH, THAT truth will SET YOU FREE from chaos and corruption because you are, NOW, carrying a REFLECTION OF THAT TRUTH THAT WILL REFRAME the chaos into the TRUTH THAT YOU ARE CARRYING, SPEAKING AND REFLECTING ... FROM YOUR POSITION!

Because Abraham SAW his blueprint and engaged it, not only did it change his body, but we see that it also changed Sarah's body! Sarah became one of the most beautiful women on the face of the earth at HER AGE ... which was NOT when she was in her "prime"! Did the hands of "time" turn back? I encourage you to go and ask God to show you for yourself. Go and take a look! However, the blueprint manifested in both she and Abraham, we see that LIFE and strength come back into them supernaturally, and she got pregnant!

Abraham DARED to step OUT OF HIS TENT and into the reality of the celestial, God's reality, that carried Abraham's true blueprint, and, in it, God showed Abraham that, "My desire is for you to see what I really have for you! It is not limited to the chaos around you!" God KNEW that the one billion trillion stars that Abraham would see in the heavens, by stretching his neck to look up, from SITTING INSIDE OF HIS TENT, sitting in his human ability, which was limited, was going to make it impossible for Abraham to count them! Meaning, from that limited chaotic position, Abraham WOULD NOT SEE what God truly had for him, he would only see Hagar and Ishmael! God was saying, "Abraham, you cannot count the stars in your limited human ability by standing in the midst of chaos, trying to produce something out of your head knowledge, out of the ONLY blueprint you see that is tied to limitations because, THAT one, will bring forth chaos! Chaos births chaos! You have to COME OUT OF YOUR TENT, out of the terrestrial, all the chaos, limitations, knowledge, and sight that come with that and INTO MY arena, the celestial arena, and let ME SHOW YOU! NOW, from THIS POSITION...YOU CAN SEE AS I SEE! Now, from THIS position, TELL THE STARS IF YOU CAN COUNT THEM!

Do you understand?

You do NOT NEED to fight for yourself! No eyeball to eyeball fighting with demons, binding demons. (UNLESS YOU ARE GIVEN A SPECIFIC ASSIGNMENT FROM GOD!!!! IT IS VERY IMPORTANT YOU SEE AND UNDERSTAND THIS! THE PERSONAL DETAILS OF YOUR EVERYDAY LIFE AND LEADING IS BETWEEN YOU AND GOD! IT IS YOUR RESPONSIBILITY TO WALK OUT THOSE PERSONAL DETAILS WITH HIM. THAT IS WHY I ALWAYS STRESS THAT THIS IS ALL BASED ON RELATIONSHIP, RELATIONSHIP, RELATIONSHIP WITH ADONAI, YESHUA AND HOLY SPIRIT...AND NOT FORMULAS!)

He wants you to understand that you must ALLOW His blueprint to FIGHT on your behalf because, as it does, ALL that is connected to THAT blueprint WILL JOIN THIS WAR...FOR YOU, on your behalf, and on the behalf of your entire bloodline! Everything and everyone that is in and connected to your blueprint, ALL that is part of your inheritance, all the angelic hosts that have been assigned to you, all the Men in White Linen that are connected to you, all of the Cloud of Witnesses that are connected to you, all the stars that are connected to you, that ARE PART of YOUR inheritance, the fullness of the government of God, all the other billion, trillion, beings that are connected and are part of your inheritance, the ULTIMATE VOICE of God AND HIS DNA...your original DNA, ALL that is part of His kingdom realms, that is connected to YOU, ALL OF THAT IS FIGHTING ON YOUR BEHALF, as YOU release God's original blueprint that He has for you!

YES, the stars are ALSO fighting on your behalf! All the stars that are part of your inheritance! In Judges 5:20 we see the stars doing just that! Now, remember, these stars are NOT angels! They are STARS! This is when Deborah went to war against Sisera, and this is what the scripture says, "From the heavens, the stars fought, from their courses they fought against Sisera." NIV. All of these things are fighting for you and your bloodline, you just got to engage it and release it!

You have to understand that the realms that God wants us to function out of IS DEFINITELY OUT of our belief system (things not seen with our natural eyes), BUT it is in our spiritual ability as the NEW CREATION, as His sons of creaTIVE light!

Why do you think there is so much hopelessness and fear, suicide, gender identity issues and so many other issues we have all gone through? WE ARE NOT LIVING OUT OF OUR ORIGINAL BLUEPRINT BUT, rather, OUT OF A COUNTERFEIT, CHAOTIC ONE AND OUR SPIRIT MAN KNOWS, AND FEELS IT! Gender identity issues are a huge manifestation of this lack of knowledge of one's original blueprint. You see, our spirit man KNOWS that we were created for MORE, for something greater than what our current reality shows us, what our family says, what the doctor says, what the bank says, what the pastor says; however, we can't seem to find the "more"! Therefore, there is a huge void in us. The church does not really fill that void because it is BIGGER than just going to church! Reading the Bible does not fill it. In fact, it can make you more desperate because, again, you KNOW that what you read is true. You see all that Jesus said you are to be, and all that He is for you, but somehow it is NOT the reality that you are living and seeing manifesting in your life! Prayer the way you always have prayed, and fasting, declaring, binding, casting out demons...none of that fills this desperate cry of your spirit man for "the more"! All of a sudden, all of the above come swarming all around you, trying to make you engage with them and give them entry. You have a choice. What you do from here. At times, it may feel like you don't have a choice. That that is a lie from the enemy! DO NOT GIVE IN TO THEM, DO NOT GIVE UP! If you are dealing with any of these issues, He wanted you to read this book, now, to understand and KNOW WHAT TO DO! This IS the beginning of the NEW season for you!

Let's continue. So, all of a sudden, you may hear a message such as this, or other messages that unveil the reality of who you really are, AND HOW to start walking that out, and your spirit man seems to vibrate, screaming with joy, because it is almost like you have given him/her, fresh, cold water like to a parched person, who was dying of thirst! What your spirit man is crying for IS WHAT IT KNOWS AND FEELS IT WAS CREATED TO DO, AND BE, WHICH IS THE

GREATNESS FOUND IN ADONAI, THROUGH JESUS! That is YOUR ORIGINAL BLUEPRINT!

I pray this book has unveiled His reality to you, and that it has given you the steps of how to's, but NOW, IT IS YOUR CHOICE WHAT YOU DO WITH IT! God wants to transform the chaos in and around you into His original blueprint for you and your family, for your bloodline and seedline... NOW! "Behold, OLD things HAVE (past tense) passed away and NOW, behold, I make ALL things NEW!" So, He wants to do this NOW! However, WHEN His NOW will happen in your life, and on your behalf, totally DEPENDS ON YOU! YOU HAVE TO CHOOSE if His "NOW 'is NOW, or if His "NOW" can be 3, 5, 10, 30 years from now!!! YOU CHOOSE THE time for His "NOW" by your actions.

Let me also say this for those of you who have an inner healing or deliverance ministry. You CAN cast out the demons that are attached to a person and bring healing, however, if they do not SEE and KNOW and learn to LIVE OUT of their original blueprint, even if it is one little step at a time, SEEING and KNOWING who their really are, what God really created them to do, it is very possible that they will, again, at some point, fall in agreement with the lies of the enemy and allow that mutated, false, chaotic reality to dictated their life once again. That is why it is so important to, first, deal with demonic trading floors and teach them about their true blueprint, and how to see it, EVEN IF IT IS ONLY ONE WORD that one sees at first! Be faithful to SAY THAT WORD, proclaim THAT word, or sentence, decree that word or sentence! Faithful in the SMALL and the INCREASE, the more, WILL be shown! This is for anyone reading this book. Go with what you SEE and hear, even if it's one word!! Be faithful with that and the more you engage with Him, the more He will give you. And, once you are faithful with that, He will give and show you more.

When we understand this, and DO IT, you guys, we are going to transform in creation ALL that needs to be transformed according to His original blueprint for ALL of creation! Remember, all of creation is groaning, calling, prophesying who YOU AND I ARE, trying to awaken us out of our spiritual amnesia so we can release back to the original blueprint of God there! Why? Because we are mature sons, ordained as kings out of our mature sonship position, to administrate a priestly role, under the Order of Melchizedek, into the earth, the terrestrial arena and in the cosmos, to REFRAME chaos and destruction into TRUTH and brood or vibrate over it, the same way the Father did in the beginning, over the waters of the deep that covered the earth until what is hidden in the deep, the true original blueprint, can break forth as His light that IS IN that blueprint! ARE YOU READY?!

ON DECEMBER 20th, 2012 there was a new dispensation that was released. That is called The Order of Melchizedek and it completely supersedes the Apostolic! Why? Because The Order of Melchizedek had to do with the GOVERNMENT OF HEAVEN, NOT the government of earth. So, it is no longer about the apostolic. God is having us go past that, into the NEXT. It's about the government of God in ALL of creation, not just the church.

I'm going to end with this one scripture, Galatians 4:1 AMP. "Now what I mean to say is that as long as an heir is an immature child, though he is the heir OF IT ALL, there is no difference between him and a slave. (So, what does God tell us that we must do, in order to mature? Watch!) v2...but he is UNDER [the authority of] guardians (the Seven Spirits of God), and HOUSEHOLD ADMINISTRATORS OR MANAGERS (I want to suggest here that these are ALL that are part of the household administration of El Elyon!! Angels, Men in White Linen, Cloud of Witnesses such as King David, Enoch, Adam, Melchizedek. ALL means ALL that are part of the administration of the Kingdom realms of YOUR FATHER!) UNTIL the date set by his father [when he is of LEGAL age]. v3. So also, we, when we were children (SPIRITUALLY IMMATURE), WERE KEPT LIKE SLAVES, UNDER THE elementary [man-made RELIGIOUS OR PHILOSOPHICAL] TEACHINGS OF THE WORD. v4. But when [IN God's plan] ... (what plan? That divine plan that was once hidden that I mentioned above found in 1 Corinthians, chapter 2. The plan that has been prepared FOR THE SPIRITUALLY MATURE ONES, WHO ARE RIPE IN THEIR UNDERSTANDING! For what purpose is that plan? To LIFT US UP INTO HIS GLORY, so that as

He is, NOW, for us to also be...IN THIS WORLD!) ...the proper time has fully come (when you have gone through the process of maturity and you are ready to be presented to the Father as a mature son, to be anointed and ordained as a king out of the process of your maturity as a son). God sent His son... v5 b "that we might be adopted [as God's children with ALL rights AS fully grown members of the family]. Again, notice we are to become AS FULLY GROWN MEMBERS that have ALL rights!

As you can see, there IS a process of maturity that we must CHOOSE to go through, so that we can step into EVERYTHING that the Spirit of Adoption has brought, called the Covenant of Adoption. We can only fully engage and operate out of that, when the appointed time has come, and that time is when you are ready to be presented to the Father, as "fully grown members of the family", as mature sons!

If we do not allow this process, as you have clearly seen in the scripture above, though we are heirs of it ALL, when the enemy looks at us, when all the creation looks at us, they see NO DIFFERENCE BETWEEN US AND A SLAVE! This is HUGE! Then we wonder why the enemy always attacks us, why things always seem to go wrong for us. The problem again is that you are acting LIKE A SLAVE and the enemy bullies slaves because he knows he can! Are you going to be seen as a slave, or as a mature son? What does your original blueprint say? Stop living out of the false blueprint calling you a slave and get up in your position. See, [if even a small glimpse of] your true blueprint. RELEASE THAT AND START LIVING OUT OF THAT! Like I said, if all you see at first is one sentence, SPEAK THAT AND LIVE OUT THAT SENTENCE! Be faithful with the small. What do you have in your hand NOW...WALK THAT OUT!

In the next chapter, I am going to walk you through an activation. It is crucial for you to remember that in order for you to SEE, YOU MUST FIRST engage the desire of your heart to SEE your Father, to SEE Jesus, to build a deeper relationship with them, and with Holy Spirit. The intent of your heart is hugely important. Focus on that intent and desire! Next, you HAVE TO ENGAGE YOUR GOD

GIVEN IMAGINATION, which IS part of the eye of your spirit! In simple terms, LET YOUR IMAGINATION PAINT the desire and intent you have in your heart! IF you HAVE the mind of Christ, which you SHOULD have, then, it is NOT YOUR MIND MAKING IT UP...IT IS HIS MIND! When you HAVE the mind of Christ, His mind comes down on your mind and it melds and mends into your mind so, therefore, your mind becomes His mind, and your mind becomes one with His! So, when you are allowing your imagination to PAINT the picture of your desire and intent, it is HIS MIND painting it! Do NOT let the enemy steal this God given ability from you!

Also, your God given imagination IS ONLY A WALKER! Before a baby can walk, in order to strengthen his or her little legs, they are put in a walker, FIRST! Now, these babies will not be in a walker for their entire life, it is just for a period of time until their legs are strengthened! Do you understand? So, BE FAITHFUL IN THE SMALL, with what you have in your hands, NOW, and the increase and strength will come! As you do this, you will move on to not having to engage your imagination, but you will all of a sudden be there and engage with the Father instantaneously! REMEMBER, all the things of God are a process! We ALWAYS are moving in a growing process, from one level of glory into the next and so on. We NEVER stop moving UP, maturing and strengthening! We never stop moving from one level of glory into the next!

Well, there again, it is a choice! This means, we have to let go of the COMFORT of our last season, and total and fully trust Him to take us AGAIN into an unknown place that will stretch us ONCE AGAIN, where we once again have to let go of all the last season and grab a hold of the new. Once we finally feel like we are getting it, and we are FINALLY feeling somewhat comfortable in it, here we go again! We have to let go of that, and go to the next unknown level, and so on. ARE YOU WILLING?

Now, let me say this also. You may not see it as clear as a movie-like picture, but you may sense something. GO WITH THAT! DO NOT SECOND GUESS YOURSELF! Acknowledge what you THINK you see, or sense, or smell, or hear, and look for the next!

NOTHING IS CRAZY OR OUT THERE! TRUST HIM as He is showing you! ALLOW your desire, the desire of your heart for more of HIM, to bring the picture and acknowledge it, and let Him build on that, till you see more!

Now, I always encourage people to get in a quiet place, get comfortable and I like to play soft meditation kind of music with no words. The music I really love to use is Kimberly and Alberto Rivera. They have a lot of incredible instrumental prophetic sounds available.

Again, I want to repeat myself here because it is very important you get this, so that you can actually engage in the entire message of this book. Hear me...THIS IS NOT HARD! We make it harder than it is by our unbelief and FEAR of a demon tricking us. OH MY GOSH! Can you imagine then, if we really believe that the TWISTED, BENT, PERSPECTIVE OF OUR FATHER THAT WE HAVE? Can you imagine how He feels when we think that IF we want to connect more with Him, IF we ask HIM to lead us, He will somehow allow a demon to come trick His children and bring destruction and chaos?! Would YOU as a parent do that to your child??? Do you see what the NASTY, CRAPPY (YES, I said that word), religious spirits have done; how they have programmed us to believe CRAP about GOD, or Father???

If you have that fear, you MUST LET GO OF IT! COME OUT OF AGREEMENT with those nasty demons, get off of that trading floor, and TRUST YOUR FATHER! Again, connect with the desire, the designer to know more of the Father, the desire to know more of Jesus, the desire to step INTO the heart of Adonai, and let THAT desire paint what you will see and, BY FAITH, SET IN TO IT... ENGAGE IN IT! You have to believe like a little child. Do NOT question what He shows you...but trust and engage!

I also want to remind you again and say that the devil created NOTHING! He steals what God gave us, perverts it, and shoves it back in our face and we immediately freak out! The devil DID NOT create the imagination! He stole it from many people as they chose to give it to him, and he has used it! IMAGINATION IS VERY POWERFUL, and he knows that! That is why he wants you NOT TO

USE IT! He is pushing people to engage FANTASY, that is engaging the desires OF THE FLESH, which is totally the counterfeit of engaging your GOD GIVEN IMAGINATION which, again, has to do with engaging the desires of your heart to connect in a deeper relationship with YOUR HEAVENLY FAMILY! Remember, the Bible says that as a man THINKS (aka imagination), SO HE IS!

God gave us the imagination because He knew, due to Adam's choice of action, before Jesus, we lost the ability to GO and see Him, see the angels, see everything in His kingdom realms. But Jesus came to RESTORE what we lost through Adam, and give us once again, free entry into the Kingdom Realms of our Father! However, it is a GROWTH and a maturity process. We needed to be strengthened in our abilities one level of glory at a time! God in His wisdom knew that we would totally freak out. We would not be able to handle it if we were to see all that is around us, and what is beyond the veil, and in any other dimension. Therefore, God gave us the imagination, which is the very beginning of you seeing through the eye of your spirit. Yes, it is your mind's eye, and again, the devil DID NOT CREATE IT! IT is a literal part of your brain that has the ability to SEE beyond! GOD created it and He wants you to use it to see into all that He has for YOU! The issue is, will one engage with that "eye" in fantasy or in the God given imagination to connect MORE with God and ALL that He has for you?

If you have ever allowed the enemy to use your imagination as fantasy, just ask the Lord to forgive you. Say, "Father forgive me for allowing the enemy to use the ability you gave me to bring about things in my life that were not Your perfect will for my life, that were not things of my original blueprint. I take now the blood of Jesus and I paint over the canvas and the screen of fantasy, canceling and making every picture, painting, or movie void! I choose to get off of its trading floor and I now choose to engage my God imagination for what You have for me, so that I can see and engage with my original blueprint and a deeper relationship with You and all that You have for me!"

ACTIVATION AND ENCOUNTER

Get in a comfortable place, dim the lights maybe. Create the atmosphere for you to be able to relax and engage. I'm going to lead you, as the Holy spirit leads me, just so you can see how it's done. But, if God takes you somewhere else, please go! If God shows you something else or additional things, please do that. Again, I just want to show you how to engage, so that, next time, you can practice it and practice it until you have encounters, daily!

Again, do NOT discount anything! You may just see a small picture, GO WITH THAT. No matter how crazy it is, don't discount it. I will lead you where the Lord leads me, but, then I will want you to go with Jesus wherever He will take you and WRITE IT DOWN!

Now, get in that place where you can be relaxed and be able to engage your spirit man. Thank you, Jesus, for Your blood and all the abilities that It has given us. Jesus, I thank you that You made a way for my position to be recognized in Heavenly places, in the celestial, in the Father's heart. I speak to Your soul, to take its rightful place inside my spirit man, as my spirit man will lead, directed by the Spirit of God.

Father, I know that the Kingdom of Heaven is as close to me as the air that I breathe, so I choose to engage with that Kingdom Realm.

As you are praying this prayer, ENGAGE with your desire to SEE Him, to SEE Jesus, to know your heavenly family more, and to build a deeper relationship with them. Let that desire paint the picture. You may see the cross...look for details! How do you see it? See a portal being opened IN the cross. It is a circular opening IN the cross that is full of light! Go in it. What does it look like, and feel like? Engage with you see or sense...do not second guess.

You may see this very thin, almost transparent, veil blowing in this soft wind. Go up to it, touch it and go through the opening. Look for details! Engage all your senses. The FIRST thing you see or hear or sense, go with that! Step through either the cross or the veil. As you are crossing through, look around to see where you are. There are no mistakes that you can make. Some of you may see this beautiful expanse of a garden with beautiful trees, some are fruit trees, some are flower trees, some trees have scrolls in the branches of different colors. What do you see? Look for details! Everywhere you look you may see beautiful flowers and rich English gardens where the flowers are alive, talking, and welcoming you.

I don't want to give you too many details because I want YOU to fill in the blanks by engaging your imagination. If you are in the garden, this IS the garden of YOUR HEART, so all that you see in it, you created for you and Jesus! You and the Father! What do YOU want in YOUR garden … this place where you meet with Jesus and you walk with the Father?

Maybe you see a pathway of golden pebbles that is following along a stream of a crystal, clear river that is rushing down. What do YOU see, smell, sense? Do not hurry! Take in all the details that you can. Allow your heart's desire to paint the picture. Now, look for Jesus. Where do you see Him? What is He doing? Is He walking towards you, or are you running towards Him?

What is He wearing? What does He look like? DO NOT second guess … first thing you see. Here, I want you to now ask Him questions. I love this thing that my dear friend Christopher Carter says, "Ask Jesus a question that you would not know the answer to." So, I want you to do that, and listen! What is He saying? DO NOT doubt what you first hear! I want you now to take a few minutes and engage with Him. Ask Him questions and LISTEN. Whatever you hear and see, ask Him the next question, build on His last response.

YOU AND HIM……….

Now, let's go into the heart of the Father. Jesus is leading you, however you see Him. We are approaching this place that is FULL of white light, so bright that you can hardly see. All around this place of this brilliant light are streams of colors, all kind of colors, dancing all around, as they are inviting you to enter. WHAT DO YOU SEE? WHERE IS JESUS? What do you feel as you enter this place? Stop and absorb what you see, hear and feel.

You have entered the heart of Adonai, this VAST space of light and beauty. How do YOU see it? As you look deeper into this place, and as you feel the frequency and vibration of the pulsating rhythm, echoing throughout, look and see the different corridors or tunnels of different lights, and density, that are going in different directions. Now, you may see the Father. How do you see Him? ENGAGE your heart desire to see Him and connect with Him.

Father, I thank you the by faith it is written that I am seated with Christ Jesus IN YOU! I am NOW IN YOU, in the most INTIMATE place IN YOU! I THANK YOU SO MUCH that You have allowed me entrance into this very sacred place...the center of who you are! Oh Father, I do NOT take this lightly! I love you and I so desire to know you like I have never known you before. I desire to only do what You created me to do. I desire to bring you joy and make you proud! I desire to always put a smile on your face as I walk out the fulness of my original blueprint that you have made for me!

Father, I want the Truth from Your perspective, the celestial perspective, I want Your original blueprint from Your perspective, from the celestial, Heavenly arena, to be the only blueprint I engage, for myself and my bloodline! I want to engage with THAT voice, that framed everything OUT OF YOUR HEART, from the beginning, to brood and vibrate over me and my bloodline, over the terrestrial and REFRAME it into Your original blueprint! Please allow me to see what I need to see of my original blueprint, for this time and season.

Now, LISTEN and LOOK for what is happening. You may be directed towards a "corridor" into a dimension or vast "room" called "Blueprint Archives" or "Blueprint Library". Go in it. As you enter in and through this tunnel, corridor, into this vast space of scrolls and blueprints, look for details. What do you see? What beings are you encountering? What angels are you seeing? …What do they look like? What are they saying and how are they connected to you? Always ask questions, listen, and observe. I want you to take time in here. NOTHING that you see is wrong!

This place is a vast place, with nooks filled with scrolls, all kinds of different scrolls as high as you can see and as wide as you can see. It is like a never ending vast, huge library-like place. Ask Jesus to take you to see yours. LOOK FOR DETAILS and do not hurry.

This is time again for you to engage by faith and let Him expand your imagination to SEE and engage. Take notes of what you see. No matter how crazy it seems, go with it!

Now, I do also want to say that however much of your blueprint you are allowed to see, even if you see a "word", that word may take on the shape of what it means. This is what I am seeing now. I see some of you that have dealt with financial chaos, OR lack in the ability to live a prosperous life, vehicles breaking down, job loss, especially due the Covid situation, lack of joy or peace, and this IS the situation that God wants to you to deal with the word "abundance" as it is coming off of our blueprint and it is taking on the image of abundance, and it looks like a garment of pure gold and filled with jewels. PUT IT ON! NOW, that IS the word you will CONTINUE TO SPEAK and release over ALL areas of LACK in your life! Remember, God's words are NOT just letters written down, BUT they are LIVING BEINGS, and when you SPEAK THEM OUT, THEY COME ALIVE and bring what THEY ARE! So that garment not only is now covering you and your bloodline, but now covers all the lack in your life and family.

Father, I thank you for showing me this part of my original blueprint. Father I chose to put on Abundance as a garment as I acknowledge you, Abundance. Thank you for being part of my blueprint. I now release you, Abundance, as this garment of gold and riches of my Father, to go and not only cover me, but my entire bloodline and everything that does not mirror who you are, in my life, my family, my children, my marriage and my entire seed line! If the Lord gives you more, release that.

I also see someone's blueprint for this season, and I see the sentence come OFF your blueprint, that says, "Breaker of limitations and strongholds". I see as these words are coming off the pages, full of life and they are swirling in front of you and taking on the image of a HUGE hammer, one that looks like Thor has. Everywhere he strikes, I see pathways of lightning and lava blowing, as you would see lightning fork in the sky, illuminating all of Heaven. As it strikes, it breaks all that was struck, and not only that, but it is also melting it in the lava and lightning the strike carries. IF that is for you, do just what was done above.

What does your blueprint reveal? Engage with it. Now remember that your blueprint has the voice of the government of YHVH connected to it, it has cloud of witnesses connected to it, it has angelic beings connected to it, it has other beings that the Father created, connected to it, it has star systems connected it it, it has nature connected to it, all that is part of your inheritance is connected to it. Do you see any of these ones that are part of your blueprint? Look for Jesus to introduce you to them, ask their name, acknowledge them, engage with them, as you release this part of your blueprint! NOTHING IS IMPOSSIBLE, NOTHING IS CRAZY! THE ONLY THING LIMITING YOU IS FEAR programmed by the religious spirits. I want to leave you with this statement that I will always shout it from the rooftops. I WILL NEVER ALLOW ANOTHER MAN'S LIMITED REALITY DICTATE THE FULLNESS OF WHO I AM AND MY ABILITIES IN GOD!

Lastly, as with everything I teach, I want to encourage you to KEEP DOING THIS! Just because you did this once, or you do it for a week and a month, does not mean that now you are all done! NO! You do it and keep doing it and keep doing it! You keep building your relationship with and keep building it. You keep declaring your blueprint and keep declaring it! You keep getting off of those demonic floors and keep trading ON heaven's Trading Floors. DO NOT STOP

AT ANY ONE PLACE but keep reaching for the next step of "GLORY" in and through Him!

The Gospel of Thomas:

Translation

by Mark M. Mattison

The text is based on NHC II, 2 – the second tractate of Volume II of the Nag Hammadi Codices, a Coptic library of ancient texts dating to the fourth century. The Nag Hammadi manuscript contains the most complete copy of Thomas' Gospel discovered so far. It's a fourth-century translation of an earlier Greek text.

In addition to the Coptic manuscript, three smaller Greek fragments also came to light in the nineteenth and twentieth centuries. The Greek copies date to the third century, which proves that

Thomas 'Gospel was widely copied in antiquity. All four copies were discovered in Egypt. Scholars widely agree that the original Gospel was probably written in the Greek language in Syria in the late first or early second century, meaning it was written at least as early as the latest books of the New Testament. Gaps ("lacunae") in the manuscript are denoted by square brackets. Words in square brackets are hypothetical reconstructions based on the size of the gap, the number of letters that probably would have fit in that gap, and the surrounding context. Angled brackets denote an emendation or correction of what appears to be a scribal error, and words in parentheses are strictly editorial additions to clarify the meaning of the text. Finally, the labels of the sayings are not in the original Coptic but are provided for ease of reference.

These are the hidden sayings that the living Jesus spoke, and Didymos Judas Thomas wrote down.

Saying One:
True Meaning
And he said, "Whoever discovers the meaning of these sayings won't taste death."

Saying Two:
Seek and Find
Jesus said, "Whoever seeks shouldn't stop until they find. When they find, they'll be disturbed. When they're disturbed, they'll be [...] amazed, and reign over the All."

Saying Three:
Seeking Within
Jesus said, "If your leaders tell you, 'Look, the kingdom is in heaven,' then the birds of heaven will precede you. If they tell you, 'It's in the sea,' then the fish will precede you. Rather, the kingdom is within you and outside of you.
"When you know yourselves, then you'll be known, and you'll realize that you're the children of the living Father. But if you don't know yourselves, then you live in poverty, and you are the poverty."

Saying Four:
First and Last
Jesus said, "The older person won't hesitate to ask a little seven-day-old child about
the place of life, and they'll live, because many who are first will be last, and they'll
become one."

Saying Five:
Hidden and Revealed
Jesus said, "Know what's in front of your face, and what's hidden from you will be
revealed to you, because there's nothing hidden that won't be revealed."

Saying Six:

Public Ritual

His disciples said to him, "Do you want us to fast? And how should we pray? Should we make donations? And what food should we avoid?"

Jesus said, "Don't lie, and don't do what you hate, because everything is revealed in

the sight of heaven; for there's nothing hidden that won't be revealed, and nothing

covered up that will stay secret."

Saying Seven:
The Lion and the Human

Jesus said, "Blessed is the lion that's eaten by a human and then becomes human,

but how awful for the human who's eaten by a lion, and the lion becomes human."

Saying Eight:
The Parable of the Fish

He said, "The human being is like a wise fisher who cast a net into the sea and drew

it up from the sea full of little fish. Among them the wise fisher found a fine large fish and cast all the little fish back down into the sea, easily choosing the large fish. Anyone who has ears to hear should hear!"

Saying Nine:
The Parable of the Sower

Jesus said, "Look, a sower went out, took a handful of seeds, and scattered them.

Some fell on the roadside; the birds came and gathered them. Others fell on the rock; they didn't take root in the soil and ears of grain didn't rise toward heaven. Yet others fell on thorns; they choked the seeds and worms ate them. Finally, others fell on good soil; it produced fruit up toward heaven, some sixty times as much and some a hundred and twenty."

Saying Ten:

Jesus and Fire (1)
Jesus said, "I've cast fire on the world, and look, I'm watching over it until it blazes."

Saying Eleven:
Those Who Are Living Won't Die (1)
Jesus said, "This heaven will disappear, and the one above it will disappear too.
Those who are dead aren't alive, and those who are living won't die. In the days when you ate what was dead, you made it alive. When you're in the light, what will you do?
On the day when you were one, you became divided. But when you become divided, what will you do?"

Saying Twelve:
James the Just
The disciples said to Jesus, "We know you're going to leave us. Who will lead us
then?"
Jesus said to them, "Wherever you are, you'll go to James the Just, for whom heaven and earth came into being."

Saying Thirteen:
Thomas 'Confession
Jesus said to his disciples, "If you were to compare me to someone, who would you
say I'm like?"
Simon Peter said to him, "You're like a just angel."
Matthew said to him, "You're like a wise philosopher."
Thomas said to him, "Teacher, I'm completely unable to say whom you're like."
Jesus said, "I'm not your teacher. Because you've drunk, you've become intoxicated by the bubbling spring I've measured out."
He took him aside and told him three things. When Thomas returned to his
companions, they asked, "What did Jesus say to you?"

Thomas said to them, "If I tell you one of the things he said to me, you'll pick up
stones and cast them at me, and fire will come out of the stones and burn you up."

Saying Fourteen:
Public Ministry
Jesus said to them, "If you fast, you'll bring guilt upon yourselves; and if you pray,
you'll be condemned; and if you make donations, you'll harm your spirits.
"If they welcome you when you enter any land and go around in the countryside,
heal those who are sick among them and eat whatever they give you,
because it's not what goes into your mouth that will defile you. What comes out of your mouth is what will defile you."

Saying Fifteen:
Worship
Jesus said, "When you see the one who wasn't born of a woman, fall down on your
face and worship that person. That's your Father."

Saying Sixteen:
Not Peace, but War
Jesus said, "Maybe people think that I've come to cast peace on the world, and they
don't know that I've come to cast divisions on the earth: fire, sword, and war. Where there are five in a house, there'll be three against two and two against three, father against and son and son against father. They'll stand up and be one."

Saying Seventeen:
Divine Gift
Jesus said, "I'll give you what no eye has ever seen, no ear has ever heard, no hand
has ever touched, and no human mind has ever thought."

Saying Eighteen:
Beginning and End
The disciples said to Jesus, "Tell us about our end. How will it come?"
Jesus said, "Have you discovered the beginning so that you can look for the end?
Because the end will be where the beginning is. Blessed is the one who will stand up in the beginning. They'll know the end, and won't taste death."

Saying Nineteen:
Five Trees in Paradise
Jesus said, "Blessed is the one who came into being before coming into being. If
you become my disciples and listen to my message, these stones will become your
servants; because there are five trees in paradise which don't change in summer or
winter, and their leaves don't fall. Whoever knows them won't taste death."

Saying Twenty:
The Parable of the Mustard Seed
The disciples asked Jesus, "Tell us, what can the kingdom of heaven be compared
to?"
He said to them, "It can be compared to a mustard seed. Though it's the smallest of all the seeds, when it falls on tilled soil it makes a plant so large that it shelters the birds of heaven."

Saying Twenty-One:
The Parables of the Field, the Bandits, and the Reaper
Mary said to Jesus, "Whom are your disciples like?"
He said, "They're like little children living in a field which isn't theirs. When the

owners of the field come, they'll say, 'Give our field back to us.' They'll strip naked in front of them to let them have it and give them their field.

"So I say that if the owner of the house realizes the bandit is coming, they'll watch
out beforehand and won't let the bandit break into the house of their domain and steal their possessions. You, then, watch out for the world! Prepare to defend yourself so that the bandits don't attack you, because what you're expecting will come. May there be a wise person among you!

"When the fruit ripened, the reaper came quickly, sickle in hand, and harvested it.
Anyone who has ears to hear should hear!"

Saying Twenty-Two:
Making the Two into One
Jesus saw some little children nursing. He said to his disciples, "These nursing
children can be compared to those who enter the kingdom."
They said to him, "Then we'll enter the kingdom as little children?"
Jesus said to them, "When you make the two into one, and make the inner like the
outer and the outer like the inner, and the upper like the lower, and so make the male and the female a single one so that the male won't be male nor the female female; when you make eyes in the place of an eye, a hand in the place of a hand, a foot in the place of a foot, and an image in the place of an image; then you'll enter [the kingdom]."

Saying Twenty-Three:
Those Who are Chosen (1)
Jesus said, "I'll choose you, one out of a thousand and two out of ten thousand, and they'll stand as a single one."

Saying Twenty-Four:
Light
His disciples said, "Show us the place where you are, because we need to look for

it."

He said to them, "Anyone who has ears to hear should hear! Light exists within a
person of light, and they light up the whole world. If they don't shine, there's darkness."

Saying Twenty-Five:
Love and Protect
Jesus said, "Love your brother as your own soul. Protect them like the pupil of your
eye."

Saying Twenty-Six:
Speck and Beam
Jesus said, "You see the speck that's in your brother's eye, but you don't see the
beam in your own eye. When you get the beam out of your own eye, then you'll be able to see clearly to get the speck out of your brother's eye."

Saying Twenty-Seven:
Fasting and Sabbath
"If you don't fast from the world, you won't find the kingdom. If you don't make
the Sabbath into a Sabbath, you won't see the Father."

Saying Twenty-Eight:
The World is Drunk
Jesus said, "I stood in the middle of the world and appeared to them in the flesh. I
found them all drunk; I didn't find any of them thirsty. My soul ached for the children of humanity, because they were blind in their hearts and couldn't see. They came into the world empty and plan on leaving the world empty. Meanwhile, they're drunk. When they shake off their wine, then they'll change."

Saying Twenty-Nine:

Spirit and Body
Jesus said, "If the flesh came into existence because of spirit, that's amazing. If spirit came into existence because of the body, that's really amazing! But I'm amazed at how [such] great wealth has been placed in this poverty."

Saying Thirty:
Divine Presence
Jesus said, "Where there are three deities, they're divine. Where there are two or one, I'm with them."

Saying Thirty-One:
Prophet and Doctor
Jesus said, "No prophet is welcome in their own village. No doctor heals those who
know them."

Saying Thirty-Two:
The Parable of the Fortified City
Jesus said, "A city built and fortified on a high mountain can't fall, nor can it be
hidden."

Saying Thirty-Three:
The Parable of the Lamp
Jesus said, "What you hear with one ear, listen to with both, then proclaim from
your rooftops. No one lights a lamp and puts it under a basket or in a hidden place.
Rather, they put it on the stand so that everyone who comes and goes can see its light."

Saying Thirty-Four:
The Parable of Those Who Can't See
Jesus said, "If someone who's blind leads someone else who's blind, both of them
fall into a pit."

Saying Thirty-Five:
The Parable of Binding the Strong
Jesus said, "No one can break into the house of the strong and take it by force
without tying the hands of the strong. Then they can loot the house."

Saying Thirty-Six:
Anxiety
Jesus said, "Don't be anxious from morning to evening or from evening to morning
about what you'll wear."

Saying Thirty-Seven:
Seeing Jesus
His disciples said, "When will you appear to us? When will we see you?"
Jesus said, "When you strip naked without being ashamed, and throw your clothes
on the ground and stomp on them as little children would, then [you'll] see the Son of the Living One and won't be afraid."

Saying Thirty-Eight:
Finding Jesus
Jesus said, "Often you've wanted to hear this message that I'm telling you, and you
don't have anyone else from whom to hear it. There will be days when you'll look for me, but you won't be able to find me."

Saying Thirty-Nine:
The Keys of Knowledge
Jesus said, "The Pharisees and the scholars have taken the keys of knowledge and
hidden them. They haven't entered, and haven't let others enter who wanted to. So be wise as serpents and innocent as doves."

Saying Forty:

A Grapevine
Jesus said, "A grapevine has been planted outside of the Father. Since it's
malnourished, it'll be pulled up by its root and destroyed."

Saying Forty-One:
More and Less
Jesus said, "Whoever has something in hand will be given more, but whoever doesn't have anything will lose even what little they do have."

Saying Forty-Two:
Passing By
Jesus said, "Become passersby."

Saying Forty-Three:
The Tree and the Fruit
His disciples said to him, "Who are you to say these things to us?"
"You don't realize who I am from what I say to you, but you've become like those
Judeans who either love the tree but hate its fruit, or love the fruit but hate the tree."

Saying Forty-Four:
Blasphemy
Jesus said, "Whoever blasphemes the Father will be forgiven, and whoever
blasphemes the Son will be forgiven, but whoever blasphemes the Holy Spirit will not be forgiven, neither on earth nor in heaven."

Saying Forty-Five:
Good and Evil
Jesus said, "Grapes aren't harvested from thorns, nor are figs gathered from thistles, because they don't produce fruit. [A person who's good] brings good things out of their treasure, and a person who's [evil] brings evil things out of their evil treasure. They say evil things because their heart is full of evil."

Saying Forty-Six:

Greater than John the Baptizer
Jesus said, "From Adam to John the Baptizer, no one's been born who's so much
greater than John the Baptizer that they shouldn't avert their eyes. But I say that
whoever among you will become a little child will know the kingdom and become
greater than John."

Saying Forty-Seven:
The Parables of Divided Loyalties, New Wine in Old Wineskins, and New
Patch on Old Cloth
Jesus said, "It's not possible for anyone to mount two horses or stretch two bows,
and it's not possible for a servant to follow two leaders, because they'll respect one and despise the other.
"No one drinks old wine and immediately wants to drink new wine. And new wine
isn't put in old wineskins, because they'd burst. Nor is old wine put in new wineskins, because it'd spoil.
"A new patch of cloth isn't sewn onto an old coat, because it'd tear apart."

Saying Forty-Eight:
Unity (1)
Jesus said, "If two make peace with each other in a single house, they'll say to the
mountain, 'Go away,' and it will."

Saying Forty-Nine:
Those Who Are Chosen (2)
Jesus said, "Blessed are those who are one – those who are chosen, because you'll
find the kingdom. You've come from there and will return there."

Saying Fifty:

Our Origin and Identity
Jesus said, "If they ask you, 'Where do you come from? 'tell them, 'We've come
from the light, the place where light came into being by itself, [established] itself, and appeared in their image.'
"If they ask you, 'Is it you? 'then say, 'We are its children, and we're chosen by our
living Father.'
"If they ask you, 'What's the sign of your Father in you? 'then say, 'It's movement
and rest.'"

Saying Fifty-One:
The New World
His disciples said to him, "When will the dead have rest, and when will the new
world come?"
He said to them, "What you're looking for has already come, but you don't know
it."

Saying Fifty-Two:
Twenty-Four Prophets
His disciples said to him, "Twenty-four prophets have spoken in Israel, and they all
spoke of you."
He said to them, "You've ignored the Living One right in front of you, and you've
talked about those who are dead."

Saying Fifty-Three:
True Circumcision
His disciples said to him, "Is circumcision useful, or not?"
He said to them, "If it were useful, parents would have children who are born
circumcised. But the true circumcision in spirit has become profitable in every way."

Saying Fifty-Four:
Those Who Are Poor
Jesus said, "Blessed are those who are poor, for yours is the kingdom of heaven."

Saying Fifty-Five:
Discipleship (1)
Jesus said, "Whoever doesn't hate their father and mother can't become my disciple, and whoever doesn't hate their brothers and sisters and take up their cross like I do isn't worthy of me."

Saying Fifty-Six:
The World is a Corpse
Jesus said, "Whoever has known the world has found a corpse. Whoever has found
a corpse, of them the world isn't worthy."

Saying Fifty-Seven:
The Parable of the Weeds
Jesus said, "My Fathers 'kingdom can be compared to someone who had [good]
seed. Their enemy came by night and sowed weeds among the good seed. The person didn't let anyone pull out the weeds, 'so that you don't pull out the wheat along with the weeds, 'they said to them. 'On the day of the harvest, the weeds will be obvious. Then they'll be pulled out and burned.'"

Saying Fifty-Eight:
Finding Life
Jesus said, "Blessed is the person who's gone to a lot of trouble. They've found life."

Saying Fifty-Nine:
The Living One
Jesus said, "Look for the Living One while you're still alive. If you die and then try

to look for him, you won't be able to."

Saying Sixty:
Don't Become a Corpse
They saw a Samaritan carrying a lamb to Judea. He said to his disciples, "What do
you think he's going to do with that lamb?"
They said to him, "He's going to kill it and eat it."
He said to them, "While it's living, he won't eat it, but only after he kills it and it
becomes a corpse."
They said, "He can't do it any other way."
He said to them, "You, too, look for a resting place, so that you won't become a
corpse and be eaten."

Saying Sixty-One:
Jesus and Salome
Jesus said, "Two will rest on a couch. One will die, the other will live."
Salome said, "Who are you, Sir, to climb onto my couch and eat off my table as if
you're from someone?"
Jesus said to her, "I'm the one who exists in equality. Some of what belongs to my
Father was given to me."
"I'm your disciple."
"So I'm telling you, if someone is <equal>, they'll be full of light; but if they're
divided, they'll be full of darkness."

Saying Sixty-Two:
Mysteries
Jesus said, "I tell my mysteries to [those who are worthy of my] mysteries. Don't let
your left hand know what your right hand is doing."

Saying Sixty-Three:

137

The Parable of the Rich Fool
Jesus said, "There was a rich man who had much money. He said, 'I'll use my money to sow, reap, plant, and fill my barns with fruit, so that I won't need anything.'That's what he was thinking to himself, but he died that very night. Anyone who has ears to hear should hear!"

Saying Sixty-Four:
The Parable of the Dinner Party
Jesus said, "Someone was planning on having guests. When dinner was ready, they
sent their servant to call the visitors.
"The servant went to the first and said, 'My master invites you.'
"They said, 'Some merchants owe me money. They're coming tonight. I need to go
and give them instructions. Excuse me from the dinner.'
"The servant went to another one and said, 'My master invites you.'
"They said, "I've just bought a house and am needed for the day. I won't have time.'
"The servant went to another one and said, 'My master invites you.'
"They said, 'My friend is getting married and I'm going to make dinner. I can't come.
Excuse me from the dinner.'
"The servant went to another one and said, 'My master invites you.'
"They said, "I've just bought a farm and am going to collect the rent. I can't come.
Excuse me.'
"The servant went back and told the master, 'The ones you've invited to the dinner
have excused themselves.'
"The master said to their servant, 'Go out to the roads and bring whomever you
find so that they can have dinner.'
"Buyers and merchants won't [enter] the places of my Father."

Saying Sixty-Five:
The Parable of the Sharecroppers

He said, "A [creditor] owned a vineyard. He leased it out to some sharecroppers to
work it so he could collect its fruit.
"He sent his servant so that the sharecroppers could give him the fruit of the
vineyard. They seized his servant, beat him, and nearly killed him.
"The servant went back and told his master. His master said, 'Maybe he just didn't
know them.' He sent another servant, but the tenants beat that one too.
"Then the master sent his son, thinking, 'Maybe they'll show some respect to my
son.'
"Because they knew that he was the heir of the vineyard, the sharecroppers seized
and killed him. Anyone who has ears to hear should hear!"

Saying Sixty-Six:
The Rejected Cornerstone
Jesus said, "Show me the stone the builders rejected; that's the cornerstone."

Saying Sixty-Seven:
Knowing Isn't Everything
Jesus said, "Whoever knows everything, but is personally lacking, lacks everything."

Saying Sixty-Eight:
Persecution
Jesus said, "Blessed are you when you're hated and persecuted, and no place will be
found where you've been persecuted."

Saying Sixty-Nine:
Those Who Are Persecuted
Jesus said, "Blessed are those who've been persecuted in their own hearts. They've

139

truly known the Father. Blessed are those who are hungry, so that their stomachs may be filled."

Saying Seventy:
Salvation is Within
Jesus said, "If you give birth to what's within you, what you have within you will
save you. If you don't have that within [you], what you don't have within you [will] kill you."

Saying Seventy-One:
Destroying the Temple
Jesus said, "I'll destroy [this] house, and no one will be able to build it […]"

Saying Seventy-Two:
Not a Divider
[Someone said to him], "Tell my brothers to divide our inheritance with me."
He said to him, "Who made me a divider?"
He turned to his disciples and said to them, "Am I really a divider?"

Saying Seventy-Three:
Workers for the Harvest
Jesus said, "The harvest really is plentiful, but the workers are few. So pray that the
Lord will send workers to the harvest."

Saying Seventy-Four:
The Empty Well
He said, "Lord, many are gathered around the well, but there's nothing to drink."

Saying Seventy-Five:
The Bridal Chamber
Jesus said, "Many are waiting at the door, but those who are one will enter the bridal chamber."

Saying Seventy-Six:
The Parable of the Pearl
Jesus said, "The Father's kingdom can be compared to a merchant with merchandise who found a pearl. The merchant was wise; they sold their merchandise and bought that single pearl for themselves.
"You, too, look for the treasure that doesn't perish but endures, where no moths
come to eat and no worms destroy."

Saying Seventy-Seven:
Jesus is the All
Jesus said, "I'm the light that's over all. I am the All. The All has come from me and unfolds toward me.
"Split a log; I'm there. Lift the stone, and you'll find me there."

Saying Seventy-Eight:
Into the Desert
Jesus said, "What did you go out into the desert to see? A reed shaken by the wind?
A [person] wearing fancy clothes, [like your] rulers and powerful people? They (wear) fancy [clothes], but can't know the truth."

Saying Seventy-Nine:
Listening to the Message
A woman in the crowd said to him, "Blessed is the womb that bore you, and the
breasts that nourished you."
He said to [her], "Blessed are those who have listened to the message of the Father
and kept it, because there will be days when you'll say, 'Blessed is the womb that didn't conceive and the breasts that haven't given milk.'"

Saying Eighty:
The World is a Body
Jesus said, "Whoever has known the world has found the body; but whoever has

found the body, of them the world isn't worthy."

Saying Eighty-One:
Riches and Renunciation (1)
Jesus said, "Whoever has become rich should become a ruler, and whoever has
power should renounce it."

Saying Eighty-Two:
Jesus and Fire (2)
Jesus said, "Whoever is near me is near the fire, and whoever is far from me is far
from the kingdom."

Saying Eighty-Three:
Light and Images
Jesus said, "Images are revealed to people, but the light within them is hidden in the
image of the Father's light. He'll be revealed, but his image will be hidden by his light."

Saying Eighty-Four:
Our Previous Images
Jesus said, "When you see your likeness, you rejoice. But when you see your images
that came into being before you did – which don't die, and aren't revealed – how much
you'll have to bear!"

Saying Eighty-Five:
Adam Wasn't Worthy
Jesus said, "Adam came into being from a great power and great wealth, but he
didn't become worthy of you. If he had been worthy, [he wouldn't have tasted] death."

Saying Eighty-Six:

Foxes and Birds
Jesus said, "[The foxes have dens] and the birds have nests, but the Son of Humanity has nowhere to lay his head and rest."

Saying Eighty-Seven:
Body and Soul
Jesus said, "How miserable is the body that depends on a body, and how miserable
is the soul that depends on both."

Saying Eighty-Eight:
Angels and Prophets
Jesus said, "The angels and the prophets will come to you and give you what belongs to you. You'll give them what you have and ask yourselves, 'When will they come and take what is theirs?'"

Saying Eighty-Nine:
Inside and Outside
Jesus said, "Why do you wash the outside of the cup? Don't you know that whoever created the inside created the outside too?"

Saying Ninety:
Jesus 'Yoke is Easy
Jesus said, "Come to me, because my yoke is easy and my requirements are light.
You'll be refreshed."

Saying Ninety-One:
Reading the Signs
They said to him, "Tell us who you are so that we may trust you."
He said to them, "You read the face of the sky and the earth, but you don't know
the one right in front of you, and you don't know how to read the present moment."

Saying Ninety-Two:
Look and Find

Jesus said, "Look and you'll find. I didn't answer your questions before. Now I want to give you answers, but you aren't looking for them."

Saying Ninety-Three:
Don't Throw Pearls to Pigs
"Don't give what's holy to the dogs, or else it might be thrown on the manure pile.
Don't throw pearls to the pigs, or else they might [...]"

Saying Ninety-Four:
Knock and It Will Be Opened
Jesus [said], "Whoever looks will find, [and whoever knocks], it will be opened for
them."

Saying Ninety-Five:
Giving Money
[Jesus said], "If you have money, don't lend it at interest. Instead, give [it to]
someone from whom you won't get it back."

Saying Ninety-Six:
The Parable of the Yeast
Jesus [said], "The Father's kingdom can be compared to a woman who took a little
yeast and [hid] it in flour. She made it into large loaves of bread. Anyone who has ears to hear should hear!"

Saying Ninety-Seven:
The Parable of the Jar of Flour
Jesus said, "The Father's kingdom can be compared to a woman carrying a jar of
flour. While she was walking down [a] long road, the jar's handle broke and the flour spilled out behind her on the road. She didn't know it, and didn't realize there was a problem until she got home, put down the jar, and found it empty."

Saying Ninety-Eight:
The Parable of the Assassin
Jesus said, "The Father's kingdom can be compared to a man who wanted to kill
someone powerful. He drew his sword in his house and drove it into the wall to figure out whether his hand was strong enough. Then he killed the powerful one."

Saying Ninety-Nine:
Jesus 'True Family
The disciples said to him, "Your brothers and mother are standing outside."
He said to them, "The people here who do the will of my Father are my brothers
and mother; they're the ones who will enter my Father's kingdom."

Saying One Hundred:
Give to Caesar What Belongs to Caesar
They showed Jesus a gold coin and said to him, "Those who belong to Caesar
demand tribute from us."
He said to them, "Give to Caesar what belongs to Caesar, give to God what belongs
to God, and give to me what belongs to me."

Saying One Hundred and One:
Discipleship (2)
"Whoever doesn't hate their [father] and mother as I do can't become my [disciple], and whoever [doesn't] love their [father] and mother as I do can't become my [disciple]. For my mother […], but [my] true [Mother] gave me Life."

Saying One Hundred and Two:
The Dog in the Feeding Trough
Jesus said, "How awful for the Pharisees who are like a dog sleeping in a feeding

trough for cattle, because the dog doesn't eat, and [doesn't let] the cattle eat either."

Saying One Hundred and Three:
The Parable of the Bandits
Jesus said, "Blessed is the one who knows where the bandits are going to enter.
[They can] get up to assemble their defenses and be prepared to defend themselves
before they arrive."

Saying One Hundred and Four:
Prayer and Fasting
They said to [Jesus], "Come, let's pray and fast today."
Jesus said, "What have I done wrong? Have I failed?
"Rather, when the groom leaves the bridal chamber, then people should fast and
pray."

Saying One Hundred and Five:
Knowing Father and Mother
Jesus said, "Whoever knows their father and mother will be called a bastard."

Saying One Hundred and Six:
Unity (2)
Jesus said, "When you make the two into one, you'll become Children of Humanity,
and if you say 'Mountain, go away!', it'll go."

Saying One Hundred and Seven:
The Parable of the Lost Sheep
Jesus said, "The kingdom can be compared to a shepherd who had a hundred sheep. The largest one strayed. He left the ninety-nine and looked for that one until he found it. Having gone through the trouble, he said to the sheep: 'I love you more than the ninety-nine.'"

Saying One Hundred and Eight:
Becoming Like Jesus
Jesus said, "Whoever drinks from my mouth will become like me, and I myself will
become like them; then, what's hidden will be revealed to them."

Saying One Hundred and Nine:
The Parable of the Hidden Treasure
Jesus said, "The kingdom can be compared to someone who had a treasure [hidden]
in their field. [They] didn't know about it. After they died, they left it to their son. The son didn't know it either. He took the field and sold it.
"The buyer plowed the field, [found] the treasure, and began to loan money at
interest to whomever they wanted."

Saying One Hundred and Ten:
Riches and Renunciation (2)
Jesus said, "Whoever has found the world and become rich should renounce the
world."

Saying One Hundred and Eleven:
Those Who are Living Won't Die (2)
Jesus said, "The heavens and the earth will roll up in front of you, and whoever lives from the Living One won't see death."
Doesn't Jesus say, "Whoever finds themselves, of them the world isn't worthy"?

Saying One Hundred and Twelve:
Flesh and Soul
Jesus said, "How awful for the flesh that depends on the soul. How awful for the
soul that depends on the flesh."

147

Made in the USA
Las Vegas, NV
24 March 2025